D1327162

starstruck

Published by Bloomsbury Publishing, New York and London
Distributed to the trade by Holtzbrinck Publishers

All papers used by Bloomsbury Publishing are natural, recyclable products made from wood grown in well-managed forests. The manufacturing processes conform to the environmental regulations of the country of origin.

Library of Congress Cataloging-in-Publication Data

Gross, Michael Joseph.
Starstruck : when a fan gets close to fame / Michael Joseph Gross.— 1st U.S. ed.
p. cm.
ISBN 1-58234-316-0 (hardcover)
1. Subculture. 2. Fans (Persons)—Psychology. 3. Celebrities. 4. Popular culture. I. Title.
HM646.G76 2005
306.4'87—dc22
2004030339

Portions of this book originally appeared, in different form, in the *Boston Globe*, the *New York Times*, the *New York Times Magazine*, *LA Weekly*, and *Entertainment Weekly*.

ISBN-13 9781582343167

First U.S. Edition 2005

1 3 5 7 9 10 8 6 4 2

Typeset by Hewer Text Ltd, Edinburgh
Printed in the United States of America
by Quebecor World Fairfield

starstruck

WHEN

A FAN GETS

CLOSE

TO FAME

michael joseph gross

BLOOMSBURY

starstruck

Published by Bloomsbury Publishing, New York and London
Distributed to the trade by Holtzbrinck Publishers

All papers used by Bloomsbury Publishing are natural, recyclable products made from wood grown in well-managed forests. The manufacturing processes conform to the environmental regulations of the country of origin.

Library of Congress Cataloging-in-Publication Data

Gross, Michael Joseph.
Starstruck : when a fan gets close to fame / Michael Joseph Gross.—
1st U.S. ed.
p. cm.
ISBN 1-58234-316-0 (hardcover)
1. Subculture. 2. Fans (Persons)—Psychology. 3. Celebrities.
4. Popular culture. I. Title.
HM646.G76 2005
306.4'87—dc22
2004030339

Portions of this book originally appeared, in different form, in the *Boston Globe*, the *New York Times*, the *New York Times Magazine*, *LA Weekly*, and *Entertainment Weekly*.

ISBN-13 9781582343167

First U.S. Edition 2005

1 3 5 7 9 10 8 6 4 2

Typeset by Hewer Text Ltd, Edinburgh
Printed in the United States of America
by Quebecor World Fairfield

starstruck

WHEN

A FAN GETS

CLOSE

TO FAME

michael joseph gross

BLOOMSBURY

To the memory of

JEAN ANN KOERNER GROSS
1937–2002

And why do my dreams, which should be the best part of me, why do my dreams, my wants, constantly humiliate me? . . . Hey, dream, I dreamed you.

—JOHN GUARE

Contents

Introduction

ON APRIL FOOLS' DAY, 1934, when Ray Bradbury was
thirteen years old, his family packed up and left Wauke-
gan, Illinois, for Hollywood, where his parents would
search for work, and he would spend his free time outside
studio lots with the packs of fans who collected autographs
from movie stars. Remembering those days, he told me,
"Of all of the people who did that sort of thing, I was the
only one who had a dream of the future. I had a purpose
for what I was doing. I was standing outside the wall of
Paramount Studios when I was thirteen years old and I had
a dream that I would jump over the wall and land inside
and write a picture."

About twenty years later, that dream came true. Walking down the red carpet with John Huston at the premiere
of *Moby Dick*, Ray Bradbury was shocked to see, standing
on the pavement, some of the autograph collectors he had
known as a teenager. He left John Huston's side and
approached them, hoping they would recognize him. "I
said, 'I was that crazy boy who used to stand with you in
front of Paramount.' They said, 'Oh, yes, what are you
doing now?' And I suddenly got very embarrassed and
didn't want to tell them. There was this chasm that opened
up between us, between what we had done together, what
they were doing now, and what I was doing now. And I

said, 'I worked on the screenplay.' And they said, 'Did you type it? Were you in the stenographer's department?' And I said finally, 'No, I wrote the screenplay.' And a strange and magical thing happened at that moment. Suddenly their hands shot out, and there were half a dozen autograph books in front of me, and somebody handing me a pen. I crossed the border. I was not collecting autographs now. I was giving my first ones. It made me cry. I had made it over the wall. But none of those other people had made it over the wall."

I've since repeated this story many times, to many different kinds of people. Its appeal seems to be as universal as a certain kind of fairy tale's—those stories where the misfit child who lives among the lowly finds his true place in a royal realm (and finally demonstrates his goodness by staying faithful to his roots). In Ray Bradbury's story, he cast himself as that kind of paradoxical character: both the "crazy boy" who counts himself as one of the autograph collectors, and the burgeoning Hollywood big shot who has left them behind. At one time or another, most of us have this fantasy of crossing over "the wall"— to become a star, or else the kind of person who's as evidently important as a star—in a way that simultaneously affirms our connection with our background and elevates us above it.

Dreams of crossing over from black and white to Technicolor can be so powerful that they trump common sense. Celebrities inspire self-contradiction: I know that stars and fans all live in the same three dimensions, but I still imagine there's a velvet-roped realm of existence that's more vivid than the everyday place where I live. I know that a meaningful life grows from well-chosen commitments, well cared for; and yet, I can't help but wonder if maybe celebrity offers a shortcut.

For me, Ray Bradbury's story hit home because I, too, was a "crazy boy." When I was young, I lived for the moments when I made contact with celebrities—because I hoped someday to be one. Eventually I mostly outgrew the idea that stars are higher and greater than us mortals. But, like most people, I'll almost always crane my neck if a famous face is in the room. And, like most people, I am prone to spurt apparently meaningless anecdotes if you mention stars that I've crossed paths with. Renée Zellweger? Saw her at my gym one day. Colin Farrell? Saw him at a bookstore, all by himself, on opening night of his first big movie.

And yet, if I care what you think of me, I might not tell you how it really made me feel to see them. I might not tell you that, because I saw Renée a few days before the Oscars (the year she was nominated for *Chicago*), when she looked in my direction, I had to quell a desperate urge to walk over, touch her, and exclaim, "*I know you're going to win!*"

I'd probably also keep it to myself that, when I saw Colin, I followed him around the bookstore—from far enough away, though, that he wouldn't sense my interest in every move he made. (I wasn't going to bug him, but still inside my head I contemplated lines that I could use to say hello if I were the kind of person who accosted movie stars in bookstores: "Where'd you get that shirt?" No. "Cool shirt. Where'd you get it?" No.) Nor would I tell you that I watched him find something in fiction and pay in cash (exact change). Or that, since I couldn't see the title, I went up to the soporific Goth cashier and said, "What book did that guy buy?" and fibbed, "It was such a cool cover, but I just couldn't see the title," and when the cashier checked the receipt, which didn't give the title, I asked, a little curtly, if he could please just trace the stock number, glared at him until he did, then bought myself a copy of that book and spent the whole of Friday night in my apartment reading it, because—well, because I figured that's what Colin did, and it had made me so happy to see him.

If I told you all that, you might think I'm strange. Starstruck. A fan. And everybody knows what fans are like: little people, taking vicarious relief from lonely lives in fascination with the famous.

Did you want to know the title of the book that Colin bought?

I grew up in Winchester, Illinois (pop. 1,700), the kind of farm town that people say is in the middle of nowhere, whose own residents (including my parents) always said, "The best thing you can do in this town is leave." As far back as I can remember, I was looking for an exit strategy, and when I was ten years old, I found it. Ronald Reagan was elected president, and I decided that I wanted more than anything to know him and to be like him. His television presence was so commanding and so personal that I believed his assurances that all was well with the world. He would say "God bless you" at the end of his speeches, and I could practically feel myself being blessed.

I wrote down quotes from the excerpts of his speeches that I heard on the evening news, reading and rereading them, trying to teach my voice the same warmth and confidence he exuded. I calculated that 2008 would be my first year of constitutional eligibility to run for president. I made election scrapbooks filled with my favorite photographs of Reagan; I drew political cartoons of my hero stomping on a peanut-shell-shaped President Carter and calling him "wimp."

One day my Cub Scout troop went to see Ronald Reagan give a speech in central Illinois, where he posed for photographs in the cab of a large piece of farm equipment. As he emerged from the cab, the press hollered questions at him, and I raised my voice to ask, "Would you please come shake hands with us?" Pointing to the reporters, he said, "I don't think they'll let me through." Then, as if momentarily stricken with Tourette's syndrome, feeling out of control, scared, and wonderful, I shouted, "I love you," to which the only response I got was hell from my fellow Cub Scouts for weeks.

Despite the Cub Scouts' taunts, I spent the van ride home from that troop outing marveling at the miracles I'd experienced: I had been recognized by the leader of the free world; powerful words conveying a vague truth had traveled from my brain into his, leaving him so stunned by my devotion that he was incapable of formulating the response he must have wanted to make. It was entirely possible that he, too, at this very moment on Air Force One, was replaying the scene in his head, wishing he had known what to say to me.

The "I love you" incident was the most dramatic expression of my growing need to reach out to the people whose attention, it seemed, would allow me to believe that I mattered. The people around me believed they were Nobodies, so what good were they? But if a Somebody paid attention to me, then wouldn't I be Somebody, too? I set myself a practical goal of *owning* part of the meaningful world beyond Winchester. And what better way than by getting the autograph of Ronald Reagan?

I sent President Reagan lengthy letters about my admiration for him and my plans to rise, as he did, from small-town Illinois obscurity to presidential fame. I made him a get-well card after he was shot by John Hinckley. I offered gentle criticisms of his policies on homelessness, lest he think I was a pushover. I made a Christmas ornament for the White House tree, sent it to Nancy, and asked if *she* would please ask the president to *personally hand-sign* the enclosed photograph of President Reagan riding horseback with Queen Elizabeth that I had obtained from the Official White House Photographer. For these efforts I was rewarded with a tall stack of glossy brochures with titles such as "A Child's Tour of the White House," and various items bearing the president's machine signature patterns, most of which I learned to recognize on sight.

I had a sharp eye for this kind of inauthenticity because, between the ages of twelve and eighteen, while most of my friends were learning to kiss girls and throw baseballs, I wore a small groove in the distal phalanx bone of my right middle finger by writing nearly five thousand letters to the likes of Deng Xiaoping, Madonna, and Francis Crick, and asking for their autographs. This was a productive pastime: I still have nearly four thousand autographs, most of them authentic. I got so many responses because I worked it out to a science. Most of the letters I wrote consisted of three paragraphs, designed to persuade them that I was worth paying attention to: (1) brief praise of addressee's work; (2) brief introduction of myself (my age, my hobbies, I'm a Boy

Scout, when I grow up I'm going to be president of the United States), followed by several questions, including—always—"To what do you attribute your success?"; (3) request for letter answering my questions and a signed photograph, please; Yours Truly, and etc.

A huge number of the people I wrote to were happy to indulge my fantasy. An astronaut who had walked on the moon even wrote, "I hope you'll send me your autograph someday." Dr. Seuss wished me luck in the 2008 election. Gene Wilder offered, "I owe my success to my neuroses," a word I immediately looked up in the dictionary. All of these little experiences of crossing over—of famous people paying attention to me, engaging me and making some modest effort at empathy, encouraging me to feel as if I were a part of their world—boosted my ego enough to make life in Winchester more bearable.

Everyone in town knew about my collection. The newspaper ran a front-page story about it; the Kiwanis Club invited me to speak; I visited little old ladies with names like Bertha Craver and Delfa Dunham and showed them my autograph albums while we ate Pepperidge Farm Cookies of Distinction and sipped sherbet drinks with mint sprigs through real silver straws. People said I was going places, and the autographs proved it.

My collection was also by far the most interesting topic of conversation for the college admissions officers I met. "What I'm trying to do is to collect letters with interesting content from historical figures who fascinate me," I would say, and tell how the bombardier of the *Enola Gay* had described, in a handwritten letter, his view of the mushroom cloud boiling above Hiroshima. I didn't tell them that the week before I got that letter, Cheryl Ladd from *Charlie's Angels* had sent me a fake signature and it ruined the whole goddamned day.

By the end of college, I had given up autograph collecting. When I told people about my collection, I hid its obsessive aspect behind a purposeful story that allowed me to fit in the Big World I longed to enter. After college I spent a few years in seminary and working in politics, and the star-struck kid inside me seemed to have faded away. I used the autographs to help me get the job I always wanted: starting out as a freelance writer, I sold some of my collection when I had trouble paying bills.

Parting with those autographs made me start wondering about the crazy boy I used to be: where he came from and where he's gone—and why, when I cross paths with famous people, he sometimes springs so quickly back to life. Though I'd stopped collecting autographs, I'll probably never leave fandom behind. My early experience as a fan formed habits of character—how I judge myself, how I judge other people—that have changed as I've grown older, but have stayed with me in subtle and not-so-subtle ways.

How about you? Think about the stars you've loved. Put your crazy crush on Kurt Cobain, Duran Duran, or Mary Tyler Moore next to the one I had on Ronald Reagan. Compare your secret, prized *Tiger Beat* scrapbook, or the way you'd line up your *Star Wars* figures on the bedspread just to look at them, with my albums full of autographs. Remember how good it made you feel, and how completely effortless it was, to be Mr. Rogers's neighbor. Or the time when you moved to a new town and it took a while to make friends, and how, in the lurch, *Friends* reruns did an okay job of filling the gap. Think about the way that your favorite rock stars always seem to be singing to *you*.

Then consider how every one of these crushes and daydreams and unrealistic hopes is a part of the story of the actual ambitions, achievements, loves, and fears that determine the course of your life. How each one is part of the wall between significance and insignificance that you've built to reach, or to stop yourself from realizing, some actual dream that you have. And how each one helps determine your status in society—identifies you (or could mark you, if the secret gets out) as the *kind of person* who likes Bruce Springsteen, or Britney Spears; Stanley Kubrick, or *Star Trek*.

Where did you put that sequined Michael Jackson glove you had in junior high? Or the Dylan concert ticket stubs, the *Dukes of Hazzard* lunch box, the Shirley Temple doll, or the T-shirt you were wearing the day you got a hug from Ringo Starr? When we grow up, most of us become embarrassed by these things and by the dreams they enshrine. In time, the memorabilia gets thrown out with the trash or maybe sold on eBay or, most often, stowed in the darkness of a closet. The emotions are harder to dispose of, even if they're easy to ignore.

We are always ignoring them. This may sound absurd in a world where celebrities seem to be everywhere. But the faces that we pick out from the blur—our favorite stars—give us a kind of pleasure that we almost never bother to describe. Few people like admitting, even to themselves, that they are starstruck.

And for good reason. If you think of yourself as even moderately informed, you are probably under the impression that fandom is a shallow, empty, or corrupting occupation of the mind. Most accounts of the culture of celebrity describe fans as deviants: obsessed loners or faceless members of hysterical crowds. Social critics claim that, in a world where technological advances have hastened moral and spiritual decay, traditional bonds of family and community have loosened, and alienated individuals have sought an artificial sense of purpose and belonging in irrational fixations on celebrities. Fans, according to this story, risk getting lost in a world where the lines between reality and fantasy erode and disappear.

In this view, fandom is at best a kind of laziness—the little people's way of imagining big life—though a laziness that's always potentially malign. The critic Neal Gabler, in *Life: The Movie* (1998), noted that "[Mark] Chapman admitted that he almost walked away from [John] Lennon with an autograph rather than Lennon's life; it was an admission of the continuity between wanting to own a small piece of a celebrity and wanting celebrity itself." Richard Schickel, in *Intimate Strangers* (1986), suggested that stalking and assassination "are far from being aberrations, given the workings of the celebrity system in our time. They are, instead, the logical end products of that system." The influence of such claims has been enormous. Almost every time I tell someone that I am writing about relationships between stars and fans, I'm asked, "Do you mean stalkers?"

I don't. At all. When people ask this question, I tell them that stalking is symptomatic of severe mental illness, and it's not related to my topic. Those who seek to hurt or kill famous people should no more be called fans than those who hunt their former spouses should be called lovers.

Granted, fandom is far from the pinnacle of well-adjustment. Fans tend to be compulsive and are almost always lonely—no one writes five thousand letters to famous people because he has inner peace and lots of friends—and fans almost always suffer frustrated ambition or desire. But psychos, they are not.

When I make this little speech, people are usually relieved. They almost always confide a story of some brush they've had with fame—the day they met Meg Ryan or got Tom Hanks's autograph—and what those moments of mutual recognition meant to them. Their initial question, though, suggests a strange fear of their own emotional response to stars, a fear they've been taught by the cognoscenti. If you want the world to think you're sane and smart, you shouldn't call yourself a fan. "Starstruck" is the opposite of intellectual, sophisticated, rational, and fulfilled.

Our culture holds this experience in such casual contempt that it isn't even recognized by the most authoritative reference work in our language. *Starstruck*—the word that best describes the emotional state in which I spent my entire adolescence, the word that describes the way that millions of people have felt upon meeting the famous people they admire—does not appear in the *Oxford English Dictionary*.

When I found that lapse, I called an editor of the dictionary, who said that she was "mortified" by the omission. Perhaps, I suggested, we could get some sense of how the *OED*'s editors understand this word by checking to see whether it appears in contextual quotes for other terms. She found two: *muddle-pated* (an English colloquialism that means "muddleheaded") and *motherfucker*.

Other dictionaries are a bit more generous. The *American Heritage Dictionary* defines *starstruck* as "fascinated by or exhibiting a fascination with fame or famous people." (The same source defines *fascinate* as "to hold an intense interest or attraction for" or "to hold motionless, spellbind." The root of *fascination*, Latin *fascinare*, "to cast a spell on," comes from *fascinum*, "an evil spell" or "a phallic-shaped amulet.")

At first glance, this seems a fairly comprehensive definition. It is broad enough to encompass the range of triggers for the feeling, which can be highly specific (if Cher's the only one who rocks your boat) or quite expansive (if you light up at the mere aura of fame: "I think she's *somebody*"). A picture in a magazine can make some people starstruck; others get the feeling only when they see stars in the flesh; and still others can be starstruck just from watching searchlights at some distant gala sweep the sky.

The spellbound connotation suggests the physical quality of the experience, and its irresistible and at least mildly incapacitating nature. (You are starstruck if you just can't help but look; you are starstruck if you faint.) Spells take many forms: sometimes the starstruck feeling starts and ends in the experience of *seeing* a celebrity; or it can move you to make your house into a Dolly Parton museum or ride public transportation for five hours to spend five minutes with Winona Ryder. As if spellbound, the starstruck fan undergoes a kind of transformation—a star, or stardom, *strikes* you, and you are, at least for the moment, a person changed.

None of this, however, accounts for what I believe to be the crucial aspect of the experience. Before I started looking up *starstruck* in the dictionary, I jotted down two definitions of my own:

To be *starstruck* is to experience *pleasure* in the presence of celebrity.
A *fan* is one who is inclined to feeling starstruck.

At its core, fandom is about pleasure, even when that pleasure is inseparable from pain or pathology. For example, although fandom is almost always a substitute for more conventional emotional fulfillment, it *works* as a substitute because it provides experiences of pleasure that make a person feel happy.

When I saw Colin Farrell, I had just moved to Los Angeles, and I knew exactly three people in the city. I spent most weekend nights doing solitary things like browsing bookstores and going to movies by myself. Seeing Colin Farrell cheered me up because I was a lonely guy, and his was a familiar face—a face that symbolized a world of fame I could briefly imagine I was part of—even though I spent the rest of the evening reading in my apartment, and I haven't ever seen that guy again.

When he left the store, my thrill at seeing Colin dissipated, my vitals stabilized, and I was left with an odd mixture of feelings: a mild burn of insufficiency, some indignance at my own desire—*what's so great about him, really?*—and a glow of contentment from having been reminded that the world is full of beautiful, surprising things.

Since the age of Alexander, the West has been preoccupied with fame, although the meaning of the concept has changed drastically since ancient times. As Leo Braudy explained in *The Frenzy of Renown: Fame and Its History* (1986), the classical world viewed fame as "a way of honoring what aspired to be permanent in human action and thought, beyond death and all of life's accidents." His book describes fame's evolution through the advent of Christianity, the fall of monarchies, the rise of modern democracy and totalitarianism, and advances in communications technology—photography, movies, television, and the Internet—that, in the twentieth century, have created a world of "fame without history." In this world, the link between fame and posterity has been broken, "questions of lasting value seem irrelevant or precious, and the audience becomes lost in an everlasting now, in which all varieties of fame are reduced to their most immediate form—whose choicest model is the performer." But Colin Farrell is no Alexander. Contemporary fame "has nothing to do with the memory of significant achievement beyond its use in future trivia quizzes. But it still pretends to wear the crown of the fame of the past. There are two worlds now: the media world and all the grand things that happen in it; and the world of normality, which seems constantly shrinking in significance."

The Frenzy of Renown is a brilliant synthesis of Western history and a sober account of the psychological and political dangers of the contemporary preoccupation with the famous. However, the closest Leo Braudy came to suggesting remedies for the problems that he diagnosed were a few remarks along the lines of "it's about time for a rebirth of personal honor and responsibility in which people no longer need to substitute their heroes for themselves."

One way to counter this culture of fame without history is for each of us to reckon with the role that fame has played in our personal history. For many people, dreams of the famous and the world they live in play at least as powerful a role in the formation of character as do our relationships with friends and family, our religion, and our place of origin. And yet because our relationships with stars are largely imaginary, and because the same media that force-feed us with celebrities also teach us that fans are freaks, most people don't seriously consider the stakes and significance of their experiences as fans. "A good deal of the contempt in which dreams are held," wrote Sigmund Freud, "is due to their preference thus shown in their content for what is indifferent and trivial." The same goes for our waking dreams.

A few years ago, I decided to start diving in the shallows. Although my adolescent lust for fame was omnivorous, Hollywood was always the focus of my fantasies. So I moved there to spend time with people who gaze upon, press against, straddle, guard, burst through, and look back on Ray Bradbury's Wall of Fame. Although I did not admit it to myself at the beginning, I also came here to see if Oz was my true home: to meet and maybe even get to know celebrities, and find out whether some time in the Technicolor world would make me happier than I had been before.

This book is the account of a three-year adventure that took me from Sundance to Dollywood, from Neverland to Middle Earth, following the trajectories of fandom through my own and other people's lives. It does not offer anything remotely like a unified-field theory of fandom, nor a balanced survey of the experiences of fans, or of celebrities, according to categories of gender, class, ethnicity, age, or sexual orientation. Instead, it tells a story about how fans and stars form relationships to sort out (or avoid confronting) the conflicts between their dreams and realities, and what sweet, sad fun people have when they set out to find the secrets, beauty, and significance that seem to exist in the world of fame. Above all, this story describes what happens when a fan gets close to fame: the exploitation, appreciation, hope, and disappointment that are contained in the pleasure of being starstruck.

From autograph collectors to entertainment journalists, to publicists, to celebrities themselves, every character in this book is part of an elaborate economy of admiration that involves every player in Hollywood's carnival of fame. What holds them all together goes back to Ray Bradbury's story: they all make the Wall of Fame the defining boundary of their lives.

Their stories, and mine, and yours, comprise one larger story about one big American dream: behind the Wall of Fame, celebrities inhabit a different world from the ordinary world where most of us live. Ronald Reagan is in there, with Dolly Parton, Mickey Rourke, and Shirley Jones, and all the famous people you've ever seen or heard of, the living and the dead. If you have some outstanding gift—star looks, comedic timing, a great voice—maybe you can join them. If you do not, then you will stay outside and watch. And if you are like the autograph collectors and the reporters on the red carpet, you're glad to, even if it makes you angry, too.

The characters in this book—and even the fact that I'm writing this book—show that we can do a lot of things with our dreams about the stars. We might as well consider those options, if we're going to keep spending so much of our leisure time consuming images of pretty and powerful and talented people.

We wouldn't spend so many hours this way if we weren't really happy that they exist. The world would be poorer without Katharine Hepburn's laugh, Janet Jackson's abs, Groucho Marx's eyebrows, and George Clooney's chin. If that sentence means anything to you, then you already know my basic premise: that fandom starts the way love starts. Something amazing about a person gets lodged in your heart, allowing a fan to see in a star what a lover sees in his beloved: an image of life's possibilities. Those weren't just random words I hollered at Ronald Reagan.

Still, there's a big difference between love and fandom. Fans who call their feelings for stars "love" are just as misguided as the critics who dismiss fans as lunatics. In love, you get to know a person, and it usually doesn't last unless it's at least a little bit mutual. Fandom, on the other hand, is an escalating process of idealization, in which actual relationship is rare (and where it's found, is usually superficial)—an inequality of affection that, in most cases, only inflames the fan's desire. Fandom is less like being in love, than like being in love with love.

So our fantasies about stars aren't so much fantasies of love as they are fantasies *about* love. We imagine the world of celebrity as an enchanted place where a person can be loved without working for it, where famous and fabulous people bask in the glow of the world's adulation just because they are so gloriously themselves. How powerful is this fantasy? Just look at the countless people who

should know better—the Nobodies who become Some-
bodies, the fans who become stars. They work furiously to
get themselves over the Wall, only to discover that the Wall
is an endlessly receding boundary. There is no such thing
as having made it. There is no world in this world where
love no longer requires effort.

The movies' most famous expression of the dream of
crossing over from a black-and-white world into something Technicolor comes from *The Wizard of Oz*. This
probably helps to explain why, in the middle of my
autograph-collecting odyssey, Judy Garland's signature
became the one I wanted most. I scanned autograph
dealers' catalogs for years looking to purchase an afford-
able, high-quality Judy Garland item, and I will never
forget the way my throat slammed shut when I finally
saw a mint-condition, vintage signed photograph of her
for $125—a bargain, even then—at an autograph show in
a hotel near the St. Louis airport one snowy Saturday.

In the years leading up to and following that day, I
bought and traded for autographs of Billie Burke (Glinda
the Good Witch), Margaret Hamilton (the Wicked Witch
of the West), Frank Morgan (the Wizard), Jack Haley (the
Tin Man), and Bert Lahr (the Cowardly Lion). I received
letters from five surviving Munchkins and from Harry
Monty, one of the Wicked Witch's Flying Monkeys. I
wrote to Ray Bolger (the Scarecrow) to ask him if he
really thought that Judy Garland had committed suicide,
hoping he'd say no, and I received a page-long response,
handwritten on the back of my letter to him, ending, "I
think she died of a mistake made by many people. Taking
too many sleeping pills and drinking alcohol at the same
time. I'm sure she was tired and couldn't sleep." I got three

signed index cards from Mervyn LeRoy, the film's producer; and (God help me) I even wrote a fan letter to film historian Aljean Harmetz, author of *The Making of The Wizard of Oz*. Fandom is nothing if not thorough.

I built a collection of *Wizard of Oz* autographs—the leads, bit players, and hangers-on—complete, lacking only the central figure. That day in St. Louis I could not bring myself to buy the Judy Garland autograph. Not because it wasn't beautiful, and not because I didn't have the money. The best explanation I can give is that I must have known, without being able to put the feeling into words, that having Judy Garland's autograph wouldn't solve the problems I wanted it to solve, wouldn't get me any closer to being able to leave Winchester. To get anywhere close to the place I wanted that autograph to take me, I was going to have to work hard. Thinking back, I'm pretty sure that that day was the beginning of the end of my autograph collecting.

Relationships between stars and fans, from the most intense to the most casual, start, like love, with the desire to recognize what is distinctive about an individual human being, and to have one's own particularity recognized as well. When one or the other pole of that passion fades— when Nirvana stops being the one band that speaks for your generation and starts to smell like a sellout, when you realize that getting Judy Garland's autograph won't make you any more special than you already are, when you finally meet Julia Roberts and realize she's never going to be your friend—then fandom starts losing its grip. At that point, we all have a choice. We can dismiss our dreams of fame for being stunted and illusive. Or we can honor them by asking why they had such power and learn from our ersatz loves so that we can do better with our true ones.

To choose the latter doesn't mean we can't still have fun when we cross paths with Colin or Renée. After all, if your heart didn't rise up a little at the sight of a star, if you don't go a little crazy inside for the guy of your dreams, then you'd have to hate the unfairness of life. We never stop believing in the Wall of Fame, even if we know it's not real, because it's too difficult to always be aware of the actual number of walls that separate everyday life from the world of celebrity. Our fantasies about celebrity aren't pathetic, however; they're experiences of pathos—because at its root, fandom is an imperfect response to the impulse to love. That's what launches every journey toward the Wall of Fame I'm describing, even the journeys that get stalled or go wrong or end sadly. That's why every person I'm going to describe in this book is worthy of your attention, even the people that you or I might be tempted to scorn and laugh at. That's why dreams about fame aren't just the little people's way of avoiding humiliation. They're everybody's way of hoping to find the dignity we all deserve.

Ray Bradbury said that he cried outside the premiere of *Moby Dick* because he only had escaped to tell the tale: "I had made it over the Wall. But none of those other people had made it over the Wall." I've spent a lot of time wondering what about that experience might make a person cry.

When he saw the autograph collectors on the other side of the velvet rope, he ran to them, not to introduce himself as a screenwriter, but to ask if they remembered him as that thirteen-year-old "crazy boy." Their response suddenly, violently, pulled him over the Wall and made him into a different creature entirely.

They recognized him for what he had done—he had written a screenplay, which meant that he'd succeeded, he had *made it*—but in a manner that obliterated their real connection with him. They didn't hug him. They stuck out their pens and their autograph books, a gesture of recognition that was impersonal, objectifying, and uninformed. They hadn't seen the movie. They didn't know the scale of his achievement. They just knew that he was up there and they were down here and so they had to reach out, in a way that only widened the chasm between them.

After he told me this story, Ray Bradbury asked me to send him a copy of what I wrote. He recited his home address. Taking it down, my mind flashed back to an image of that same address in my own handwriting, on the envelope in which, at the end of my collecting days in college, I'd sent him my copy of his book about the writing of *Moby Dick*—a book I hadn't read, about a movie I hadn't seen and didn't know the first thing about. All I knew about it was that Ray Bradbury was famous, and I had somehow picked up the idea that this book was important, and so I needed to get him to sign it. I didn't tell him any of this. I just wrote down the address again. I didn't want him to know that I was a crazy boy, too.

1

How Much Will You Give Me?

FOR CIARRA, WINONA RYDER'S shoplifting trial was a chance to see "the best person in the whole world." She arrived at the Beverly Hills courthouse with her friend Brittni just moments after recess of the trial's final day. After the press left the courtroom but before the defendant did, the two fourteen-year-old girls told the bailiff outside the chamber the story of their journey—five bus connections in as many hours, from Canoga Park in the San Fernando Valley—and then he let them into the gallery to get a glimpse of Winona.

Although the courtroom was nearly empty, the girls sat in the last row of seats. "Omigod, she's pretty," whispered Ciarra, who has clear green eyes, flawless pale skin, and a pierced eyebrow.

"Look at us, look at us, look at us," Brittni murmured hopefully.

When the girls caught Winona's eye, they waved furiously. The actress looked delighted: she grinned, waved back, and blew them a kiss.

They approached the front of the gallery, and Winona walked over to hug them and kiss each of them on the cheek. When Ciarra introduced herself by name, Winona said, "That's my goddaughter's name!" and Ciarra replied, "I know." Two bailiffs intervened when Ciarra offered the star her notebook and an orange Magic Marker. "Can't I sign just one autograph?" Winona asked, in a voice that seemed to question the fairness of life.

They sternly shook their heads, and Winona returned to confer with her lawyer. Brittni, who had pink hair, sat down with Ciarra and said, "I will never wash this cheek." When the bailiffs wandered off, Winona beelined back across the courtroom, determined to give her autograph to the girls. Her hands were shaking slightly; she made a squiggle on the page, a false start. "Oh, I'll just make that a heart," she said, then wrote, "Thank you so much. Lots and lots of peace and love." She added a couple of CD recommendations: "P.S. Essential listening: Bright Eyes (Lifted) Wilco (Yankee Foxtrot Hotel)."

Ecstatic, the girls left the courtroom and waited for Winona to emerge, to get one more glimpse when she walked down the hallway to the elevator. While they waited, I asked Ciarra if it bothered her that Winona might be guilty of stealing, and she said, "I don't care."

As Winona walked down the hall, Brittni hollered, "I love you!"

Winona said, "I love you, too!"

Standing in the back of the crowded elevator, surrounded by her entourage, Winona held eye contact with the girls, raised her arm, made a defiant V sign with her fingers, and called out, "Peace!" Brittni and Ciarra mirrored both the gesture and the cry, and the elevator doors closed.

At that point, the girls barely knew what to do with themselves. They hugged one another. "We should go get her downstairs," Brittni said.

"No, she'll think we're weirdos," Ciarra said.

Reporters surrounded them, asking what Winona had written in their notebooks. Ciarra looked wary. She pressed her notebook to her chest and told the reporters that Winona wrote "stuff. Like, a lot of stuff. A whole page." The reporters asked to see the autographs ("I'm with *Newsweek* magazine. I could get your names in *Newsweek* . . ."), and Brittni said no, "It's personal." The reporters kept after them until Brittni interrupted, "Wait a minute. How much will you give me?"—a train of thought that led directly to "Do you think that this could get us on TV?"

Outside the courthouse, Brittni and Ciarra approached a reporter from *Celebrity Justice*, a syndicated tabloid show. "We have autographs," Brittni said, and then, in what she called her "first TV interview ever," she was asked what she thinks of Winona Ryder. "She's pretty, and she's like a role model and stuff. She touched my pen."

The girls held up their notebooks so the camera could get a close-up of the autographs that they'd been guarding with their lives just minutes earlier. Then the cameraman asked if he could shoot some "B-roll"—staged shots of people engaging in everyday activities that news producers use to make transitions in their stories. He directed Brittni and Ciarra to act natural, and they shuffled down the sidewalk side by side, at first trying to gaze casually into the distance and stifle their grins, then giving up on acting cool and just mugging their little hearts out. Brittni was wearing a backpack covered with handwritten slogans, including one, in big letters, that read LOVE SUCKS.

Within half an hour, Brittni and Ciarra had undergone quite a metamorphosis. Their sweet love for Winona

Ryder was rewarded when the actress gave them auto-graphs—unique things made to commemorate their meeting. After cherishing the autographs for about five minutes, Brittni and Ciarra realized that their treasures had trade value, and they commenced to bartering. They settled for attention, but first they asked for money.

Their story illustrates a shift in the way that fans relate to stars that has been accelerating since the mid-1980s. Fans have always objectified celebrities, but today more than ever, we commodify them, too. Anything they touch, even their half-eaten pancakes, will sell on eBay. Most people standing outside parties and premieres asking for their autographs are professionals who sell the signatures they get for almost pure profit.

Stars know this. Most of them resent it. In both formal and informal ways, they have restructured their relation-ships with fans to control what they perceive to be their exploitation. Many stars now sell their own autographs through middlemen, fan clubs, or official Web sites, or at collectors' shows. Others, like Winona Ryder, say they only sign for children—presumably because they think kids' motives are more likely to be pure.

In the early years of Hollywood, MGM and other studios taught contract players to be stars. There literally were classes where performers like Lana Turner and Judy Garland learned how to interact with fans. In-house studio fan-mail services helped them coordinate their correspon-dence. When the studio system collapsed, those classes ended, fan mail got farmed out to a few private companies, and the etiquette of star-to-fan relations began eroding, too. Jason Priestley (of *Beverly Hills, 90210*) told me, "I went to acting school where I learned the craft of acting.

But there's no craft of fan appreciation. There's no rule book. There's no guide, and no person to show you how to do it. You'd think a publicist might, but my publicist would say, 'You can have a Web site if you want one. Whatever.' That kind of stuff takes time, and I'm so busy working that I don't have time to think about how to manage those relationships."

Each star makes his own idiosyncratic decisions about managing relationships with fans or delegates someone else to make those decisions for him. I've talked to dozens of celebrities and members of their support teams about how they make these choices. Because standards of etiquette for interaction between stars and fans are such a jumble, their relationships have never been more confusing. In this ethical disarray, economic value is more openly acknowledged as a defining force in their relations. More fans trade on their passion for stars to make a living, and more stars work to squeeze profit from their celebrity.

Stars, of course, have always been commodities, and fans have always been consumers. Traditionally, neither stars nor fans have talked about the role of money in their marriage, for fear of looking crass or disturbing their mutual fantasies of love. The cultural shifts I've been describing make it difficult to avoid the topic any longer. Stars and fans are running out of ways to hide our endless cycles of vending and veneration: the infinite feedback loop of celebrity, a snake that eats its own tail.

As recently as fifteen years ago, most of the autograph collectors in Los Angeles were still true fans, according to Jan Schray, an elderly widow in North Hollywood. As a little girl in Miami, Jan kissed a photograph of Gene Autry

every night before bed, and she began collecting autographs at age eleven. "I was put into a children's home
when I was young, and my escapism was writing to stars
and getting their autographs," she told me. She arrived in
Los Angeles in 1964 and collected on and off for decades,
but her real glory days began when the original Spago
restaurant opened its doors in 1982. "Oh, that was so
wonderful," she remembered, sitting on the afghan-
covered sofa in the living room of the apartment she shares
with two cats, Angel and Bum. "*Everyone* came. I'd stand
outside there five or six nights a week."

Jan was among the first of L.A.'s autograph hounds to
turn her hobby into a job when, in 1985, to help pay
medical bills after her fourth husband's heart attack, she
issued her first catalog of "in-person" signatures. During
the next few years other fans followed suit, and as collecting turned professional, autograph hounds got greedy.
They began asking stars for "multiples"—usually two to
ten signatures, though depending on a star's patience, the
numbers can soar to twenty or higher. (When a star signs
multiples, collectors call it "racking"; a really good night is
a "rack-fest." Gene Hackman, a very willing signer, is
called "Gene Rackman.") Soon the Internet and eBay
made selling all but effortless.

As the market for contemporary entertainment signatures grew, the character of the collectors turned mercenary, and field tactics became increasingly aggressive. Jan
told me that she stopped autograph hunting in 1994
because she felt threatened and embarrassed by the new
breed of collectors-for-hire. "They weren't fans. They were
calling the stars every bad word you could ever think of. I
just didn't want to be in that company because a lot of the

stars had gotten to know me. I mean, Ann-Margret used to call me by name. I went to all her shows in Las Vegas, and she invited me backstage one time."

One dealer hired a group of seventeen- to nineteen-year-old boys nicknamed "the baseballers" (they always wore baseball caps), who might have sprung from *A Clockwork Orange*: they marked up older collectors' clothes with Sharpie pens, slashed tires, and punched and shoved anyone who got in their way. They also introduced the practice of "ripping" stars who refused to sign—hollering, insulting, and teasing mercilessly. At the Academy luncheon honoring the 1993 Oscar nominees, they made Angela Bassett cry. The original gang of baseballers is gone now, but they changed the rules of L.A.'s autograph world for good.

Young collectors such as Ben, a long-haired, rock-star-handsome guy who started collecting professionally as a student at UCLA, thoroughly internalized their ethos. (Since I first met Ben in 2001, he has dropped autograph collecting to become a paparazzi photographer, of which more later.) At times he has participated in what he calls the Beverly Hills Debeautification Program, which consists of strewing garbage over the streets of posh L.A. neighborhoods where stars live. In his view, it's a rack-or-be-ripped world: "If [stars are] bucking the system when it comes to the standard relationship between a celebrity and an autograph seeker, then I in turn am gonna buck the system and do things my way. You don't want to sign—I was being polite—now we're not signing, so we're not being polite anymore." Warming to his own aggression, he said, "Autograph collecting is married to celebrity, and if they want to dissolve that marriage, that's not valid."

In the glove compartment of his black Toyota pickup truck, Ben kept a four-page, single-spaced handwritten list of stars' license plate numbers, most of which he'd memorized. "Go ahead," he said. "Test me." He spent many days and nights driving around L.A. keeping an eye out for stars' cars, which he then followed wherever they went. Results of this technique were spotty. "Kristin Scott Thomas was all scared or whatever when we followed her home the other night," he said. One of Ben's friends who followed Mena Suvari before the success of *American Beauty* got her to sign thirty-five photographs in a Los Angeles boutique. Mena has since become reluctant to sign. "I ruined her," the friend bragged.

As stars grow wise to the autograph-collecting business, some choose to sign only one item per collector. In that case, a collector can run back to his car, make a quick costume change, adjust his posture and his voice, and go back for more. One collector's cache of disguises included a Rasta hat, a drab olive baseball cap with a stringy brown wig attached, several styles of sunglasses, and a couple of changes of clothes.

Other stars, like Camryn Manheim (once an autograph collector herself), naively think they can discourage autograph sales by placing personal inscriptions above their signatures. This is where acetone comes in: a light application of the chemical removes the inscription without damaging the photograph. For a client who wanted nude photographs signed by Robin Givens, an actress who generally refuses such requests, a collector named Steve Woolf scored a "big coup. I got a topless shot signed by her. Had to be creative for that. I took a black Sharpie and drew a bikini top on her. Then I can remove that. She would never in a million years sign that if she knew it was nude."

Surveying such tactics, a collector named Mike Wehrmann told me, "As bad as this is and as much as these guys curse and as much as these celebrities know that everybody sells, with very few exceptions almost all of them still seem to sign autographs." He explained that "signing an autograph is really the definition of being a famous person. I mean, what happens when you watch a TV movie about someone who is up-and-coming? The thing that defines them suddenly being famous is that somebody comes up and asks them for an autograph. There's a scene like that in every movie. And that's the defining moment. That's when you become famous."

The breakdown in civility between collectors and stars hastened a decline in standards of penmanship. "The young stars today, they just give you squiggles, they don't even write their names," Jan said. "Leonardo DiCaprio, I got him before he became the *Titanic* star. I mean he was wonderful. He signed everything, every letter. Now it's just two zeros."

Declining standards of penmanship led to increasing incidents of forgery. Brian Chanes of the Beverly Hills gallery Profiles in History, one of the country's most prestigious autograph dealers, said, "Look at Tom Cruise's signature, it's just *whoosh!* If you buy a movie star autograph, you are buying the reputation of the person who actually acquired it, because as far as authentication, it's shaky at best." (In May of 2000, the FBI and the U.S. attorney in San Diego announced an investigation called Operation Bullpen, a $10 million bust of forged sports autographs and counterfeit memorabilia. Three years later, Operation Bullpen scored a $150,000 bust, this time for counterfeit celebrity autographs and memorabilia. Most reputable dealers estimate that at least 80 percent of material on the market is forged.)

In a market flooded with forgeries, prices fall and competition intensifies. Jan Schray, who supplements her Social Security income with her autograph business, has seen revenues decline in recent years. "People are being ripped off so badly. They don't know what's real and what's not," she complained. "And I'm struggling because mine are real and no one cares."

Because Jan's business grew from her passion for collecting, she built a following among customers who not only want authentic signatures, but also want to share in her enthusiasm and her stories and memories of meeting the stars—all of the layers of authenticity that an autograph evokes. Now she's being crowded out of the market that she helped create. For the few collectors who value Jan Schray's brand of reality, however, she remains a valuable contact.

One customer who has become her friend is "Warhead," a.k.a. Jeff Carlock, a landscaper from Ozark, Missouri, with a heavy Southern accent and a blazing, face-wide grin. At least once a year he drives twelve hundred miles to Hollywood and crashes at Jan's apartment for as long as three weeks, collecting autographs every night and sleeping most of every day. I met Warhead the day after he met his "all-time favorite actor," an encounter he described in one unstoppable stream of glee: "He comes out of the place. I mean right there you're seeing Al Pacino, from right here to that doorway right over there, it's Al Pacino! That's not going to happen back in Missouri, so it's a pretty cool deal for me. So you see the guy, it's a guy that's brought you a lot of happiness watching some movies, it's a guy that's got a real God-given talent to do something, and he walks out of the place and he signs a few over here, and then not to be rude he goes over to the other side and signs a few, and then he needs to be going, and he's getting ready to get into the limo, and I said, 'Al, one more please?' I've got one from *Scarface*. He comes over there and puts the pen on it for me. Dots it with total Pacino style, gets in the limo, and leaves. And he just made me the happiest guy in this whole town. Standing amongst a bunch of guys who, they just can't believe they didn't get five more photos signed. They're going, 'Golly, that's only forty more dollars,' it's all cha-ching, cha-ching."

To cover the cost of his trip, Warhead sold Jan some of the signatures he got during his visit, and he kept the rest for his collection. Jan Schray relies on people like him, a select few collectors whom she trusts implicitly, to supply her with new material. But her strongest competitive advantage in the world of in-person autograph sales is her stock of signatures from the 1960s. "I've got a lot of stuff put away, like my Brandos and Liz Taylors and Barbra Streisands, some of the good names. I probably have at least forty Ronald Reagans that I've got put away, and I hate to look at it that way, you know, but let's face it, that's kind of like money in the bank." She has set aside about a thousand index cards signed by stars who are deceased or soon to be so. She keeps them in a brown card file in her storage closet labeled "Dead."

*   *   *

I started collecting autographs when I made the chance discovery in my mom's address book of a sheet of paper on which were written the addresses of several famous people (including Bob Hope and the cast of *Little House on the Prairie*) whom she had contacted to request donations for an auction to benefit a local archaeological site.

Although I had already begun my quest for Ronald Reagan's signature, it hadn't occurred to me that I could collect autographs from all kinds of people until I found these addresses. On Mom's list, the star that most appealed to me was Melissa Gilbert (Laura on *Little House*). For most of my childhood, *Little House* and *The Waltons* were the only prime-time shows I was allowed to watch, and Laura's well-meaning, bungled efforts to be a good kid (which so often met with misunderstanding, which made her feel angry and act ornery) were easy for me to identify with.

I write all this in hindsight, but I'm sure the letter that I sent her conveyed some of these thoughts. I wanted Melissa Gilbert to know that I was like her (or like Laura, which I thought were the same thing), and that she was like me, and it seemed true to me that if I got her autograph, then I would have some proof of our connection.

In about a month, I received a five-by-seven manila envelope in the mail. Carefully I opened it and found a color photograph of the cast standing outside the Ingalls cabin. On first glance, it looked to have been signed not just by Laura, but by all of them. In the light of our dining room window, I made hungry inspection of the picture and was fairly devastated to discover that the signatures were fake. They didn't float on the surface; there was nothing spontaneous or sloppy or human about them. They were printed, inert, stamped into the image—a falsity that struck me as a stinging rejection. It also excited my desire for the real thing.

Maybe, I thought, Melissa Gilbert really was ornery. Maybe Pa was the nice one.

Off went another letter, to Michael Landon. Same response. Same dumb picture, same fake autographs. I wrote to each cast member: Karen Grassle (Ma), Melissa Sue Anderson (Mary), Lindsay and Sidney Greenbush (Carrie). I figured that if I went low enough on the list, someone would give me the real thing. I was wrong, and it made me angry, which made me act a little ornery.

Through interlibrary loan, I ordered a book about autograph collecting, in which I read that a handwritten, signed musical quotation from *West Side Story* by Leonard Bernstein was worth $150—a massive amount of money for a twelve-year-old in 1982. I had never heard a song from *West Side Story*. But I hoped that if I said the music was great (which would not, strictly speaking, be lying. Its reputation was great, and its reputation was all I knew) and I was in seventh grade and I played it on the piano all the time (a lie, but one that I could live with), Leonard Bernstein would probably send me a handwritten musical quotation like I saw in that book.

I was right. One week later a tiny envelope from the New York Philharmonic arrived in my mailbox. Having been once bitten, I feared opening the envelope. I took it into the dining room and held it up to the light, which revealed exuberant scribblings all over a three-by-five card, which I pulled out with a sense of triumph completely out of proportion to my interest in Leonard Bernstein.

Melissa Gilbert be damned, I kept writing letters. I spent

long hours at the library, copying down addresses from *Who's Who in America*. I subscribed to autograph collectors' magazines, which provided me with dozens of home addresses for obscure celebrities such as silent-film stars, Eastern European astronauts, and professional hockey players. I had never seen a silent movie or an ice rink, but I found myself developing a preoccupying need to obtain some piece of the life of almost every famous person who came to my attention.

Although my first impulse to get an autograph came from admiration for a star, receiving those fake signatures complicated my motives. I still wrote to people that I truly admired, and even now I treasure some of the responses I received, like a corking little note from Marlene Dietrich and a long letter from Maximilian Schell. Increasingly, however, I just wanted to prove that I could get past the people who were guarding against my message getting through, to actually get stars' personal attention.

Letters announcing my outlandish presidential ambitions, I found, were almost always good for a rise. I also made quick studies of people's backgrounds so that I could make informed comments about their work and ask unusual questions that might engage them; but few of my letters really said much more than *I want to be like you*. (Or, since I was telling them that I wanted to be president, I suppose I was actually saying, *I want to be bigger than you*.) As I look back, it seems strange to me that they elicited such lively responses from so many people. That the prince of Liechtenstein and Jackie Gleason were sufficiently flattered by this kind of letter to take the time to respond suggests that perhaps they possessed a craving for recognition, and a capacity for delusion, that might have rivaled that of my teenaged self.

Every once in a while, my abstract admiration for a celebrity elicited some real engagement. Stephen Sondheim, Keith Haring, and Olivia de Havilland were among those who wrote thoughtful letters suggesting that my attention mattered to them, in each case triggering ongoing correspondence. Their responses provoked me to learn more about each of them, which led me to enjoy some extraordinary work they'd done. It took a long time to track down a videotape of *The Heiress* in central Illinois in 1986, but hearing Olivia de Havilland speak the movie's devastating final line—"Yes, I can be very cruel. I have been taught by masters"—made the search worthwhile.

Mostly, I collected autographs because they made me feel less lonely. To me, autographs had the kind of power that medieval Christians ascribed to relics of the saints. With something like reverence, I believed they conveyed the real presence of their subjects. A signed picture of Bette Davis represented a moment of her precious, famous, coveted attention, and I had seven signed photographs of Bette Davis—which mitigated the fear that I was a nobody in the middle of nowhere. It didn't matter so much that I always got picked last for dodgeball if I could create a reason to believe that I might someday be on a first-name basis with movie stars.

After Leonard Bernstein, though, my drive to collect was also always about getting things from stars that were worth money. When Tom Brokaw would announce that a celebrity had died, I was always much sadder for the loss if I didn't yet "have" the star. I didn't sit around wishing stars would die, but I did feel pleasure if the expiring celebrity was one whose signature I had. I knew that was kind of sick, but I couldn't help it. As everyone kept telling me, and as I kept reminding myself, "This stuff is going to be worth something someday."

In the dark of the parking garage of his Los Angeles apartment complex, thirty-five-year-old Mike Wehrmann was digging through the trunk of his rented, anonymously respectable black Mercury Grand Marquis. A pretty young woman approached, unabashedly flirting. "Every time I see you, you're looking in your trunk," she said playfully. "What's in there?"

He glanced at her, blushed, looked back in the trunk—at three thousand unsigned photographs, four electric guitars (you never know where Sting'll pop up), and assorted sports equipment (for those days when he runs into Arnold Palmer, say, or Muhammad Ali).

"Just a few bodies," Mike said, still looking in the trunk, then turned to make eye contact again, but by now the woman was almost at her car, both hands on her purse.

Mike Wehrmann is embarrassed by his job. He is also probably the best in the world at what he does. Mike, who lives in New York and spends winters in L.A., is widely recognized for being the first to apply paparazzi techniques (car chases, stakeouts) to autograph collecting. "The first person I started chasing was Michael Jackson, when I was seventeen. Every day, wherever Michael went, I would go there." (Michael Jackson is generally a reluctant signer, but Mike baits him with barter: "I give him photos. Like Elizabeth Taylor photos and Shirley Temple photos. He loves that. You hold up a Shirley Temple, he'll come, like, running over.") While staking out the King of Pop, Mike became friendly with paparazzi photographers who taught him the tricks of tracking—how to cultivate sources inside restaurants, clubs, airlines, and limousine services to help him keep tabs on the comings and goings of the world's most famous people.

They also got him wondering whether autograph collecting, which he'd been hooked on since a fateful Mets game in 1979, might be a good way to make some cash. When Mike started selling signatures, at seventeen, the business brought him more than money. "It legitimized me with the photographers, and even with myself. Now I had an excuse to go out more, because there was a real purpose to it, as opposed to being a kid who's just running around. I wanted to set out to conquer the whole thing if I could." He has been pulling down six figures annually since his early twenties. (Part-time collectors can make at least $20,000 a year working just three or four nights a week.)

Watching him in action, it's clear that the relationship between autograph collectors and celebrities isn't simply parasitic. It's symbiotic. For celebrities, autograph hounds provide a specific kind of acknowledgment that is central to the experience of stardom. Mike has succeeded in this business largely because he knows how to give stars the attention they crave in order to get the autographs he wants.

Over the years, with tact and good timing, he's built professional relationships that are both solid and surreal. "When Keith Richards signs, he always tells me, you know, raspy voice, 'Keep the prices up,'" and "Andy Warhol used to stop and talk for, literally, a half hour on the street. He wanted to know everything—who's nice, who's not nice." Still, Mike has no illusions about the depth of these connections. He invoked the inevitable analogy: "It's sort of like hunting. People hunting. You're out there for your prey."

Which is to say, Mick Jagger didn't have a chance.

One January afternoon, Mike got a tip that Mick Jagger would be leaving L.A. on the four-thirty American Airlines flight to New York. We left Mike's apartment at two-forty-five and pulled into a spot in an LAX parking garage one level above the arrival area at about three-twenty. From this vantage point, Mike could keep an eye on the curbside check-in without being spotted, either by other collectors (who would know that if Mike is there, it's a big one) or by the greeters who escort VIPs to their gates. He spent the next half hour pulling photos of Mick Jagger from his trunk, peeling protective plastic off the guitars, testing pens on an old copy of the *Hollywood Reporter*, peeking down at the curb every few minutes, and calling "an associate" in New York (another collector, who, on a tip from Mike, would drive to JFK and catch Mick upon arrival).

Then he handed me a folder full of eight-by-tens and we walked to the check-in area. Mike is good-looking, nicely built, with thick brown hair parted down the middle and feathered back. In denim shorts, a baggy printed T-shirt, and beat-up white leather Asics, he had the casual vitality of a laid-back Little League coach—except for the three bright red electric guitars he was carrying.

At three-fifty, as a Lincoln Town Car with tinted windows pulled over, Mike Wehrmann got on his game face: his neutral expression softened, his close-set brown eyes widened, and the little worry wrinkle next to his left eyebrow almost disappeared. His mouth formed the mild, close-lipped smile of a happy child. You wouldn't want to let him down.

Mike thrust a guitar at me as we walked outside ("Just hold it like this. I'll do the talking"), and there was no time to object because the car door opened and Mick Jagger unfolded himself onto the sidewalk, bodyguard close behind. Mike had pulled me over the line, into the position that he occupies every day—a position that I remembered well—standing in front of a star, hamstrung, weirdly, between supplication and demand.

"Hey, Mick!" he said sweetly. "Hey, Mick, can you sign two today? 'Cause it's Sunday? And we've been real good?" Mick, sour and gray, took the pen and made a bunch of vertical slashes on one of the guitars ($2,000 retail).

"Mick, since it's Sunday, and we've been real good, could you sign two?" Mike said, and pointed the rock star toward my guitar ($2,000 again).

"How about—" But Mick, in silver, thick-framed sunglasses, turned his face away. "That's all, boys. *Bon voyage*," he said with a weary French inflection, drifting past us through the door.

Mike's game face lasted most of the way home. This was a good afternoon, he admitted, but he said it was nothing like the old days: "In the eighties, Mick would come over and sign ten things no problem. He'd joke around, talk to you. Was real nice."

Mike has serious qualms about what he's doing with his life. He says he's humiliated by professional in-person collecting, which he compares to panhandling. "If you're doing it with their consent, it's a step above begging. If you do it without their consent, then celebrities think you're cheating them and lying and being deceitful. So it's kind of a lose-lose situation." His voice had the rough-edged anger of fresh outrage, so I asked him how long he'd felt this way, and he said, "Always. I remember standing outside hotels thinking this stuff when I was seventeen, eighteen, nineteen."

For the past few years, Mike has spent an increasing amount of time arranging signing deals with actors and actresses through their agents. He pays celebrities a set fee per signature, and then wholesales these items to dealers around the country. (The Universal Autograph Collectors' Club, a nonprofit association, lists more than two hundred dealers.) Such deals have been common for professional athletes since the early 1980s, but Mike helped pioneer them for entertainers. He's done deals with Little Richard, Jerry Lewis, my old pen pal Olivia de Havilland, and cast members from *Star Trek, The Honeymooners,* and *Diff'rent Strokes.* For Mike, the arrangement saves time (some stars can sign two hundred items for him in twenty minutes). More importantly, it saves face.

"When people ask me what I do, meeting women or whatever, that throws me. I still don't have a down-pat answer. I tell them more about the deals." The deals, he figures, are "a normal business. Waiting out front of some restaurant hoping somebody's in there who's gonna come out and sign your thing is not normal." *Normal* is one thing that Mike believes autograph collectors are not, and that word laces his conversation with the bewilderment of an eternal outsider. Thinking back to the parking garage, Mike furrowed his brow: "You meet somebody normal, and then they look in your trunk. I mean, would you want to have to explain?"

Like most professional autograph collectors, Mike has a habit of low-rating himself. "I think if autograph collecting were such a great thing to do, you'd have a better class of people doing it," he grumbled one day. He is articulate and introspective, but he always shut down when I pressed the question of why he's still collecting if it's always made him feel abnormal and uncomfortable. He said he'd rather not "psychoanalyze" autograph collecting because the effort would be futile. "Autograph collecting is just something to do that's kind of fun," he said. Then, more surly: "Some people collect Cracker Jack boxes. I mean, there's a lot more stupid crap you could be doing with your time."

People who do psychoanalyze collecting argue that collectors gain a fleeting sense of companionship from acquiring certain objects, and that those experiences of acquisition offer temporary relief from feelings such as shame, loneliness, or anxiety. In *Collecting: An Unruly Passion* (1994), Werner Muensterberger wrote, "It is the search—successful or not—that ever promises hope, suspense, excitement, and even danger. The quest is never-ending. It is . . . bound to repeat itself, while the ultimate pleasure always remains a mirage."

When I was fourteen, my family took a summer vacation to Washington, D.C. In the bottom of my suitcase, I carefully packed a folder containing an Official White House Photograph of the President with Indira Gandhi (which I had already sent to India, where it had been signed by Prime Minister Gandhi), in hopes that somehow I would find a way to get Ronald Reagan's autograph. During a brief, get-your-picture-taken meeting with my congressman in his Capitol office, he mentioned that he was going to the White House later that day. I pounced: whipped out the picture and made my plea.

When I returned that afternoon, his secretary told me, "When the congressman arrived, he said, 'Mr. President, before we talk, I have one order of business for you. Could you please sign this photograph?'" She handed me the picture. It was signed, and it was real.

I asked my dad to take me to get a Coca-Cola in a restaurant at Union Station near the Capitol so I could sit and look at my prize. I kept the soda as far away from the photograph as possible to protect the thing from spills and from the mist of fizzing above the liquid's surface. Dad sat across the table from me. I don't think we talked much. I was too full of amazement that I finally had a piece of my idol, a moment of his life. Almost immediately, I also thought, I wasn't there. I was not the one that got it. It was for my congressman, not for me.

I spent the rest of the afternoon going door-to-door in the Senate Office Buildings, leaving requests for signed photographs of dozens of senators, whether I had heard of them or not. The next day, I continued working the hallways until I'd stopped in every single senator's office. In the process, I learned to sense the receptionists' suspicion or their openness, and to modulate my requests to maximize my chances of getting what I wanted. It was fun, but hollow fun, learning how to make a hundred secretaries think I cared and was deserving.

Steve Woolf will tell you the best marker to use for autographs (not Sharpies, which smudge too easily; the best are Sanford Vis-À-Vis overhead transparency markers, eighty-nine cents). He'll tell you the best colors of ink to use (blue for contemporary stars—"blue is a contemporary color"; black "for nostalgia"). He'll show you how to hold photographs a certain way for southpaws (like Sarah Jessica Parker and Julia Roberts) so the autographs come out straight, and so the lefties' hands don't drag across their signatures. He thinks it's best to stake out an event to the right of the entrance, because "it's human nature to veer right."

And as a former sales manager for Dodge (he quit a few years ago to sell autographs full-time), Steve knows a thing or two about marketing. His customers are "ninety percent men," aged twenty to thirty-five; they buy autographs for themselves, not as gifts (Christmas season is slow); and their favorite products are suggestive photographs signed by young actresses, models, or *Playboy* Playmates.

Three or four times a week for more than ten years, Steve has been driving one hundred twenty miles round-trip from his home in Riverside to Hollywood, often with his wife, Yvonne, and son, Jeffrey, to collect the autographs they sell through a family business called I.P.A. Network (I.P.A. stands for In-Person Autograph). In America's cult of celebrity, Steve believes that professional autograph collectors play a crucial intercessory role: "What I am doing is a service for a lot of people out there who are unable to have personal contact with these celebrities and are willing to pay money for it. I'm the go-between." Jeffrey, who's in his early twenties, agrees: "With forgers on the rise, celebrities should be glad that people like us are giving their fans legitimate material and not conning them."

The Woolfs' vocational idealism is anchored in a straightforward economic argument, best illustrated by a showdown between Jeffrey and Kevin Costner that occurred at a golf tournament in the mid-1990s. As Jeffrey tells the story, the actor responded to his request for an autograph by saying, " 'I'm not signing that. All you're going to do is just go sell them. Why should I do that for you?' So I kind of broke out of my shell, and I'm like, 'What's the big deal, Mr. Costner? What's so bad about it? You've got your millions.' "

Jeffrey's reasoning is not groundless. In a culture where almost everyone views each person he meets as a means to some profitable end, he has a point. It seems sensible, and arguably just, that in Hollywood fandom has become professionalized. To defend that position with integrity, however, would require a kind of detachment that autograph collectors do not have.

Every professional collector I met tried to convince me that what he is doing is "just a job," and yet almost every such statement eventually broke down, because none of the collectors could hide a measure of starstruck, decidedly unbusinesslike anxiety about what the stars think of them. Jeffrey Woolf said that many stars "think you're no good. You're not a fan. They think you're the scum of the earth. Mel Gibson, Paul Newman, Jim Carrey. But we're people as well. We're people that like movies. That's why it's difficult doing this business. An example is Jim Carrey. I love his movies, but I've met him a couple times and I don't like him as a person."

Another collector named Rich, who is renowned among his peers for being the only one of their number to become friends with a celebrity—Angelina Jolie took him to Benihana for his fortieth birthday—told me one night, "Celebrities are just nobodies that everybody's heard of."

Within seconds of his making this statement, Sarah Jessica Parker walked by us and he added earnestly, "It's sort of neat to think we have cameos in these people's lives. You know, 'Cast of Thousands . . .'"

Such ambivalence among the collectors spoils any attempt to resolve the central tension of their working lives: the question of whether they're really just businesspeople or really just fans. As in almost any human relationship, there's an economy of enjoyment and use operating here. For autograph collectors, the tension between these dynamics is unusually high, because they've chosen to trade on a capacity for adoration that comes naturally to them, as to most of us—the impulse to admire celebrities—as the primary source of their personal income. When the collectors talk about the highlights of their careers, they don't mention the most valuable signatures they ever got; they talk about the times when a star crossed the line and engaged them, whether antagonistically ("Tobey Maguire hates me," Ben boasted) or sympathetically ("Angelina says she thinks it's great what I do," Rich said). Professional autograph collecting, even at its most aggressive, still expresses the enthrallment of fandom.

Courtney Love emerged one night from a party at the Mondrian Hotel on Sunset Boulevard, carrying what looked to be a double Scotch, neat. She walked directly over when the collectors called her, took a blue Sharpie pen from one of them, and signed a bunch of photos. Then, as she was about to walk off, Brian Eick, a professional autograph dealer from Las Vegas, asked her to pose for a photo with him. Instead, she took the Sharpie, pressed its tip to his chest, and slowly drew a cross over his heart on his white oxford Polo shirt, trailing the horizontal line across his torso. Brian stood immobile, chuckling a little.

Expressionless, she sketched three little hearts on his shoulder and wrote above them, "You can call me Corky!" Then she kissed him, leaving a big lipstick mark; hugged him; beamed for the cameras; turned and sashayed to her limousine. One man who still had an unsigned photo called out to her, "Courtney! Please come back! Just one more!" She showed no sign of hearing him.

"I'm from Seattle!" he called out.

Before getting in her car, she looked up, tossed her blond hair, and said in a tone spiked with disdain, " 'I'm from Seattle'? What does that mean? 206? *Fuck.*"

Courtney began the encounter by playing her role, in response to the collectors playing theirs—the star signing autographs for her fans—and then she overstepped her bounds by taking the pen to the shirt: *I'll do what I want to do, not just what you ask me to.* After she crossed that line, people stopped asking for autographs and started taking pictures. Finally, getting into the limousine, she gave their heads a pound against the Wall of Fame, as if she'd only been pretending the encounter was sublime: *Seattle? You are* not *a part of me.* That way, the next time she saw them, she would still be the star—approachable yet untouchable—and the collectors would know their place, as fans.

After Courtney left, Brian Eick looked confused. He tried to wipe Courtney's lipstick off his cheek but succeeded only in smearing it around. "Damn," he said tentatively, as if unsure of his feelings. Then he seemed to decide he was a little angry. "This is just about my favorite shirt."

Everyone was quiet for a second. Somebody said, tough

and hopeful, "Get three hundred bucks for that on eBay." There was a general murmur of assent. Brian cracked a smile.

All night, as more collectors showed up at the Mondrian, Brian got to tell his Courtney Love story over and over. Nobody could remember anything quite like that ever happening before, and everybody said that it was cool.

As autograph collecting has become a profession, star-fan relationships have generally grown more distant and commercialized—to a point where it would be almost impossible for a kid in Illinois today to build the kind of autograph collection I put together as a teenager. During my sophomore year of high school, John Larroquette (from *Night Court*) called me on the telephone one night during supper to ask how I got his home address. I described to him my favorite book, *The Ultimate Movie, T.V., and Rock Directory*, explaining, "It has twenty thousand addresses for stars like you."

As I talked, he said "How bizarre" at least four times. A week later, I received a long handwritten letter from him and a couple of signed eight-by-tens.

Today, most celebrities say they throw away all fan mail that comes to their homes. Mail sent to studios, record labels, and publicists is generally funneled to a few private companies that "take care of fan mail so stars don't have to," as Sean Hayes (of *Will & Grace*) explained the situation to me. Although he uses a fan mail service, he said he didn't know which one.

Many stars share Sean's perspective on fan mail: they know that it exists, but they don't seem to know much about it. At the premiere of *The Last Samurai*, I asked Tom

Cruise whether he had employees dedicated to answering fan mail or developing an official Web site, and he said, "You know, they work on stuff like that. People answer fan mail. And, you know, I don't know about the Web site. Web sites, there are so many of them out there."

I put the question more concretely: "What happens to a piece of fan mail that goes to Tom Cruise?"

He said, "They send 'em in, and they go through and they read it, and they'll write things back to them. That's kind of what happens."

I tried another angle. "How much of it do you actually see?"

"I don't know. There's so much that comes in sometimes. I always try to answer a lot of them back, but sometimes they send them to the wrong address."

This confused me, but I continued, "Are there any letters that you've kept?"

Teeth clenched, he gave his jaw muscles a ripple. "There are some very moving letters."

About twenty years ago, in her garage in Sherman Oaks, Mackie Mann launched a fan mail service called The Mail Mann. At that time she had one computer and one client (Peter Reckell, from the soap opera *Days of Our Lives*). Today there are five computers in the garage, and Mackie and several employees answer between thirty thousand and forty thousand letters and e-mails per month for about one hundred clients. In 1995, she launched a subsidiary called Celebrity Merchandise, an Internet company that sells tchotchkes and coordinates fan clubs for stars including Brian Wilson of the Beach Boys and Elvira, Mistress of the Dark.

When I asked Mackie how much fan mail is forwarded to celebrities themselves, she answered, "None." Then she backpedaled a bit, adding, "There are some clients who ask for—like if it's [from] a terminally ill child, that gets passed on to them. Or if it's gifts, those get passed on." A few of Mackie's clients, such as Elvira, are very involved with fan mail and insist on signing all their own autographs. Others, Mackie said, "don't even know who we are." And some celebrities "hire us to read their mail just to check to see if there are any crazies out there. They don't want us to answer it."

The proportion of "crazies" in the mail bins, she said, comes to "half a percent. Mostly, it's just kids that want pictures. Or want to communicate. There's someone who sends flowers every week to Paula Abdul."

Then there is the e-mail. Today, fans can request photos with facsimile signatures of some stars just by clicking a button on a Web site and providing a street address. The ease of these requests has increased Mackie's gross receipts (she charges a fee of at least seventy-four cents per item shipped). It's also made her job more mechanical and impersonal. In recent years, it's gotten to the point where she never even meets some of the celebrities whose mail she's hired to answer, such as Anna Paquin and Rob Lowe. "I don't know if you want to write that," she said, "but it's the truth."

Her main competitors in the business are Spanky Taylor, a woman in Burbank whose twenty-five clients include Ben Affleck and Charlize Theron; and Jack Tamkin, whose Studio Fan Mail is the oldest and likely the largest of the three companies. Jack, whose company made the *Little House on the Prairie* photograph that ignited this whole obsession for me, declined my repeated requests to interview him—which counts as proof, in my opinion, that there is order in the universe.

All three make good livings, but none of them have any status in Hollywood. For most celebrities, Mackie said, the people who answer fan mail are "really the last ones on the totem pole. They have agents, managers, business managers, publicists. It's the last thing they think about." Before the Internet, celebrities "seemed to understand the importance of fan mail, because they didn't have any other medium to communicate directly with the fans. It makes me sad because of how it's changed. I'll change with it. But it does kind of make me sad."

The Internet has not only changed fan mail; it's transforming the whole experience of fandom. Many journalists have described the Internet's usefulness for galvanizing groups of fans into "communities" of appreciation or activism (Cast This Person; Don't Cancel That Show), and fans have staked out warrens on the Web where they build shrines to entertainers or publish "fanfic" (imagined stories about favorite stars or franchises).

The Web is also working subtler, more pervasive changes in the way that stars and fans relate to one another—by exaggerating the paradox of distance and intimacy that makes mass entertainment compelling to begin with. The Internet offers fans experiences of virtual engagement that first seem intimate, but ultimately prove alienating, largely because stars are learning to charge money for tokens of those experiences. Today, fans are paying plenty more than the price of a postage stamp for the honor of enjoying the idea that they're in contact with the stars.

* * *

The world of actors' Web sites is full of foul surprises. Plug "courteneycox.com" into your browser and you'll find yourself at the gateway of "Club Pink" ("Warning! No children allowed!"). Kathybates.com offers pictures of Asian women in negligés promoting something called Club Hong Kong. I found no similar domain squatters using male stars' names. If I had, I would have told Alyssa Milano's mom.

In 1998, when Alyssa (the star of *Charmed* and *Who's the Boss*) was awarded a $230,000 judgment against a Web site that posted nude photographs of her without her permission, Alyssa used the money to create a company called SafeSearching, to help celebrities set up official Web sites and protect their names and images from being used as tastelessly as hers had been. SafeSearching works with another company called CyberTrackers to do a search and destroy (with cease-and-desist orders) on unauthorized Internet celebrity porn. When I spoke with Alyssa's mother and manager, Lin Milano, who is the CEO of both companies, she said, "I love celebrities. I have a kid that's a celebrity. It's very important that we teach celebrities to empower themselves and show their fans who they really are and take their names away from the basement webmasters.

"A star's name," she explained, "is theirs. It's what they give to the world. It's the only thing they have."

With four employees tending about fifty stars' official Web sites (including those of Justin Timberlake, Diane Lane, and Tyne Daly), SafeSearching.com is the largest celebrity Web developer I've found. The sites look slick, and they fulfill the company's snore-inducing mission to provide "controlled and professional presentation of celebrity content," as described in its business proposal. Famous names are pretty much the only thing of value these sites have.

Each greeting message reads like an amateur press release. ("An actress whose acclaimed career has bridged childhood stardom with classic leading lady status, Diane Lane continues to impress with each new performance.") Here and there you'll find a scrap of pseudopersonal reflection, such as the Q&A about "the holidays" at ToriSpelling.com ("Q: What's the most thoughtful gift you've ever given? A: The most thoughtful X-mas gift I've ever given was serving meals to the homeless at The Los Angeles Mission"). On Tori's site, I clicked the button that said "Get an authentic autographed photo!" and was fed back to SafeSearching.com's store, where the only available autograph was Alyssa Milano's—for $49.95, plus $10 shipping and handling.

Outside the oxygen-free network of SafeSearching, actors and actresses have created some fascinating sites, many of which are built by people who actually know them well. In 1997, for example, when Sir Ian McKellen was in Los Angeles to film *Gods and Monsters*, he asked his friend Keith Stern, a computer consultant, to create mckellen.com, a shaggy collection of Sir Ian's writings and photographs that is a treasure trove of contemporary Shakespearean and sci-fi lore, and the actor's political activism.

In his small, memorabilia-crammed office above a Thai restaurant on Sunset Boulevard, Keith explained, "As people do in this town, whether you're a masseur or a nanny or a yoga teacher, you get passed around. So when Brendan Fraser and Lynn Redgrave saw what I'd done for

Ian, they were both very interested to have me do the same for them, so I did redgrave.com for Lynn and brendanfraser.com for Brendan."

When Keith went to New Zealand to visit Sir Ian on the set of the *Lord of the Rings* films in May of 2000, the same thing happened again. "I was spending my days going from hotel room to hotel room trying to help people out in various ways, making sure Orlando was able to get orlandobloom.com, helping Billy Boyd get billyboyd.net, and Sean Astin and Andy Serkis both developed Web sites with me."

Keith said he's never been approached by a manager or publicist to launch a Web site because "publicists and managers are still suspicious of the Web. They don't like its directness, and they think of it as being in competition with or a distraction from the work they do." All of his work has come from personal acquaintance with celebrities. As a result, his sites have a rambling, this-is-my-letter-to-the-world quality. Lynn Redgrave probably shouldn't have put so many personal photos up, Sean Astin's poetry is humid as a rain forest, and Sir Ian's essay on the death of Ronald Reagan could do with some blue pencil. And yet in every case, you're glad they overshared. Their Web sites convey a complexity of character that traditional media don't have time or space to describe. You could watch *E! News Daily* until your eyes fell out, and you'd never learn as much about these stars as you'll find here.

Other celebrities' official sites deliver the same sense of intimacy, with better production values. Clicking through JeffBridges.com, I had the sense that I'd got hold of the actor's diary, filled with sketches, pithy aphorisms, tips on how to build a labyrinth on your lawn, and cool stuff about parrots. The elaborately hyperlinked LilyTomlin .com weaves many of her best characters into an adventure of associations: at the end of one string of links, there's an image of Ernestine the phone operator, and every time you click on her, she snorts. Hallewood.com also gave me a snort or two. In the section called "Halle's Workout," I watched QuickTime movies of the Academy Award winner doing crunches and running on a treadmill. The button marked "Inner Beauty" ("Click here to enter Halle's Heart") led to marginally more mindful fun. There, Halle Berry responds to queries like "It seems like you don't identify with the white side of your heritage . . . why is that?"

The sense of familiarity inspired by celebrity Web sites is, however, limited and short-lived. After an hour on LilyTomlin.com, I couldn't find any way to leave a message or request an autograph. Searching for the same possibilities on Hallewood.com, I was asked to pay $39.95 (plus shipping and handling) to join Halle's fan club, the Groovers. As a Groover, I'd get access to a "Yahoo VIP Message Board" where Halle might read or respond to my postings, and I would receive a "pre-printed" autograph. (Groovers also get a Halle baseball cap, a Halle mouse pad, a Halle sticker, and entries in her "VIP Only Contest," to win "Phone Calls, Movie Premiere Tickets AND Visits to meet Halle on the Set!") Eventually I found a way to buy the fake autograph à la carte for $12. (An unspecified "portion" of money spent at Hallewood goes to charity.) For Sean Astin's signature, I was sent to the Web site of a company called Autographed to You, where, for thirty bucks, I could choose from four photos and ten possible inscriptions (like "Believe in your dreams" and "Dare to dream").

Check out Autographed to You and you'll find a lot of dreams for sale. Like signed pictures of Barry Williams (Greg on *The Brady Bunch*) inscribed "You're groovier than Marcia," which will set you back another thirty bucks. Or a twelve-second audio clip of Ruth Buzzi ("Hi, I'm Gladys Ormphby, star of *Laugh-In*. If you don't leave a message, I'll hit you with my purse!") for your answering machine. That's $27. (Eight-by-tens of Ruth licking a fish—no explanation is provided—inscribed "Best Fishes" are $21.) And signed glossies of James Carville (yes, this has been proofread) are another $30 per. Be warned: the Web site won't accept orders for autographs unless customers specify a proper name for personal inscription. (That way, they're harder to resell.) And just in case you start suspecting something less than honorable is going on here, almost every screen shot of the site bears this reassuring text block: "It's for a good cause! Because the celebrities we feature care about their loyal fans, and about the world we live in, 33.3% of every dollar earned will be donated to the celebrities' favorite charities."

As a grown-up, I know that actors' Web sites, like their performances, excite desires they cannot satisfy. I know that Halle Berry, for example, is busy, especially since she won that Oscar. I also know that Halle Berry is a private person, and that the only thing she truly owes her fans is good work. Still, if Halle's cool with letting any random fan watch her do chest presses, I think it's strange that she's cagey when it comes to autographs. A signature is, arguably, a normal thing to want from a movie star; a front-row seat to watch her abs routine is, arguably, a pervy thing to want.

Halle, though, apparently believes that it makes sense to satisfy voyeurs for free, then charge $12 for a fake signature. In her world, a fan club membership is worth a full day's pay at minimum wage. Though I'd love to know how she chose these price points, Halle's publicist says that she's too busy to discuss.

Let me be completely clear: Halle really is unusually generous to her fans. (I can't imagine Nicole would deign to set up an official fan club, much less invite one of the unwashed to visit her on set unless maybe you were ten years old and terminal.)

Halle is also systematically means-testing fans, charging $43.90 (including shipping and handling) for a place in Hallewood's ninth circle. Then again, my perspective on this kind of commerce may be skewed. I'm a guy who used to write to Katharine Hepburn—also a fairly busy, private person, and an Oscar-winner (four times over)—who always wrote me back and never asked me for a penny.

Web sites, fan clubs, and fan mail services all buffer the commercial qualities of interactions of celebrities and fans. Even big-game autograph hunters often try to hide the mercenary character of their relationships with stars. At collectors' shows, however, fandom's commerce parades in public absolutely naked.

Most years, on the morning of the Golden Globes, while people like Sean Penn and Charlize Theron are rehearsing their acceptance speeches, people like Howard Keel and Charlotte Rae are hauling boxes of their old head shots into the Grand Ballroom of Beverly Garland's Ramada Inn on Vineland in Studio City. There, at the triennial Hollywood Collectors' Show, they spend the day sitting at folding tables signing pictures and selling them to hundreds of fans who travel from as far away as Australia and Germany for these events. (Photos go for $15 to $30; most stars charge set fees of $10 to $25 to sign posters, pictures, or memorabilia that fans bring along with them to the show, and roughly the same amount to pose for snapshots.)

I've been to the show three times now; as I entered the ballroom on my first visit, I saw Jon Walmsley (who played Jason on *The Waltons*) sitting next to two of the Munchkins from *The Wizard of Oz* (who periodically sang songs from the movie), who were kitty-corner from Jay North (*Dennis the Menace*), who was just down from Felix Silla, who played Cousin Itt on *The Addams Family*, who was around the bend from Lou Ferrigno (*The Incredible Hulk*), who was five seats over from Corey Feldman (who is almost exactly my age), who was across the aisle from Shirley Jones (who once won an Oscar).

Outside, a group of collectors planned their attack. There was a brief fracas over whether to ask for Jerry Maren's autograph. One man deftly combined economic arguments for prestige and scarcity: "He's, like, the most famous Munchkin. And he's not gonna be around much longer." Another considered: "He's in the Lollipop Guild, yeah?" A third sensed an opening and made Jerry Maren a must-have: "He's the one with the lollipop itself."

Eddie Munster, whose name is Butch Patrick (but whose real name is Patrick Lilly), stood at the door puffing on a cigarette and answering strangers' questions, such as "How's Yvonne DeCarlo?"

"Fine," he said, exhaling smoke. "She's fine."

The wreckage can be riveting. Heading back into the ballroom, I found Karen Lynn Gorney, the star of *Saturday Night Fever*, who told me that she was trying to raise money to record an album of songs written by her father: "He wrote 'Brother, Can You Spare a Dime?'"

Then I watched a skinny, hearing-impaired guy who looked to be in his early twenties tell Shirley Jones, with considerable effort, "I saw you in the Hollywood Christmas Parade."

"Yes," she replied patiently in a taking-compliments tone, "it was a wonderful parade."

Thrilled by her acknowledgment, his mouth smiling through every difficult word of his next question, the man asked, "Have you ever been to the Tournament of Roses Parade?"

Assuming he wanted to hear more about her parade credits, Shirley Jones began to explain that she'd been in that one, too—and was interrupted when he said, "You can smell all the flowers," smiling bigger and more joyfully than before.

There was a terrible long pause, and, as if convicted of narcissism, the actress breathed a barely audible "That's right."

If I were Shirley Jones, I might have gone home and stuck my head in the oven after that. She told me that she would spend the evening with her arm packed in ice, to reduce the swelling from spending the whole day signing autographs.

Mixed in with such brutality, the Hollywood Collectors'

Show also has the generous, homesick feeling of a family reunion. It is a place where fading stars and their admirers go to remind themselves of what they once meant to each other, a place where almost everyone agrees to ignore each other's failures and losses, and to concentrate on recapturing the pleasures of the past. It's a place where almost anyone can feel important for a while, regardless of their status in the outside world.

Dorothy DeBorba, an *Our Gang* player who made her last film seventy years ago, is now about eighty years old, living in Livermore, California. At the show, she sold photographs depicting herself in sixteen different poses, and she said that she expected to clear about $300 for ten hours' work plus two days of unreimbursed train travel. (Most stars at the show, especially TV stars from the sixties and seventies, make considerably more—from $1,000 to $20,000.) She showed me a bouquet of flowers wrapped in grocery-store cellophane that one fan had given her. "Think of all the love that comes through here," she said. "It really is a form of applause."

Margaret Kerry, the live model for Tinker Bell in Walt Disney's *Peter Pan*, sat at her table surrounded by half a dozen fans. She was wearing black pants and a sweater jacket with silver sparkly fibers woven in, and her clear glasses frames had little bits of silver confetti in them. She was once a guest star on *The Andy Griffith Show*, and one man asked her what that experience was like. She said, "Those who were regulars, supporting characters, were on the perimeter of the main stars in the center, and those who were guest stars were on the perimeter of that. We would wait for shooting to start, and then it was like, 'Okay, now it's time!' and then Don Knotts would come in and say, 'O-

kay!' and clown around and give us all that wonderful
Mayberry feeling. The best thing was, you never felt like an
outsider, which is very important when you go in to play a
small part."

And Robert Pine, a character actor who's been in everything from *The Day of the Locust* to *Six Feet Under*, and
who's probably best known as Sergeant Joseph Getraer on
CHiPs—Erik Estrada's boss, the avuncular, frustrated guy
who ran the meetings at CHiPs headquarters—told me late
one afternoon that his face was tired from smiling. All day,
people brought photos of him that he had never seen
before. Someone even brought his CHiPs uniform shirt
to sign. The tips of his fingers were grimy from handling
money.

This was his first visit to the Beverly Garland, and he
couldn't quite make sense of these fans shelling out their
money for his autograph, of all people's. "I mean, Mickey
Mantle, that's an icon. We are a con," he said. "You learn
a lot of humility when you do a thing like this. You get to
feeling like your career isn't where it should be. You're not
a Redford or a Kevin Spacey. And all you have to do is turn
around, and there's a fucking sea of people who would like
to be where you are."

Of those fans, he said, "They are uncynical. I've met
some very nice people today that you might at another
time laugh at. It's easy to pick people out and put them
down because they dress funny. But why? Why do that?"

One of those people, a fat lady with thick legs and bright
eyes, told me, "I'm here for Hayley Mills, because I always
wished that I could go to camp and find the twin that I
never knew I had."

*   *   *

The Hollywood Collectors' Show was created by Ray and Sharon Courts, both in their mid-fifties. When Ray was growing up, his family owned a Chrysler dealership near Hurricane, West Virginia, where Sharon lived. Ray worked in an ice cream shop and met Sharon there when she came in for a treat in 1970. As it turned out, they were both movie fans—Sharon used to fantasize that she was Annette Funicello, and Ray used to fantasize that he was Troy Donahue, kissing Annette Funicello. They got married seven months later, and a few years after that, when Ray decided he didn't like cold weather, they moved to Florida. By this time, Ray was selling 16mm films by mail and at memorabilia shows, and Sharon, a housewife, helped him run the business. As they traveled around the country to these shows, they noticed the popularity of celebrity guests, which got Ray thinking that a whole show with celebrities as the central attraction and memorabilia dealers on the side might be a hit. Thirteen years later, they've mounted more than seventy-five shows in Hollywood, Ft. Lauderdale, San Francisco, New York, and Chicago.

Their Web site (www.hollywoodcollectorshow.com), which plays the theme song from *Happy Days*, lists the guests for recent and upcoming events, with biographical notes in the warm yet gossipy style of a small-town newspaper: "On October 22nd, we were notified . . . that Jay R. '*Freckles*' Smith, from Hal Roach's '*Our Gang*' / '*The Little Rascals*', was found *murdered*, in Apex, Nevada," begins one entry. "As most of you know, Jay. R., for the past 4 years, was a semi-regular at our Show. Our family would like to send our prayers and love, as well as our sympathy, to Jay's family."

Through the years, Ray and Sharon have had about fifteen hundred celebrities come through their shows, generating a revenue stream that allows them to live well. "We have a big swimming pool and a nice little spread with room for our horses," said Ray, a Southern Baptist with a bristly mustache and round spectacles. Sharon, a steel magnolia, is just as folksy as her husband, but a tad more brisk. Their business model is simple. Revenue comes entirely from ticket sales—$30 for early birds, allowed into the ballroom at 8 A.M., and $15 for general admission, beginning at 10 A.M. (most of the stars head home to ice their arms at about 5 P.M.)—and from space rental for memorabilia dealers. Celebrities, who keep 100 percent of the proceeds from their signings, receive table space for free. "We've never even taken a nickel from our celebrities," Ray said. "You see us go around with soft drinks and coffee and water for them? We've got Sharpies when they run out of Sharpies. It's all free."

Over breakfast at the Ramada one morning, Sharon explained that a few stars (Charlton Heston, Janet Leigh) have donated all of the proceeds from their sales to charity, but that many of the show's celebrity guests are on fixed incomes, and some, such as the former Munchkins and the *Our Gang* players, receive no residuals for their work. Such celebrities have told Ray, "This is how we get by for the next couple of months." He shook his head with pity. "It's a lot of pressure on us."

At the show, stars and fans alike show gratitude to Ray and Sharon. While we were talking, one fan approached the table to say, "I've been waiting for this all year. Thanks for keeping up the good work." When he was out of earshot, Sharon said, "It makes us feel so good that we can do something that gets so many compliments. A lot of times you do things in life and you don't even get acknowledged.

"I mean, we even have people want our autographs." Her voice dropped to a stage whisper. "It's *amazing*. I say, *Why*? They say, 'Cause you're the *promoters*."

Ray confessed, "It was like that guy yesterday, he had a photo of me and him that he blew up to an eight-by-ten and he brought to me—and I *signed* it." Still, Ray quickly added, he doesn't let the adulation go to his head. "We're just peons," he said. "We love meeting the stars as much as anybody."

Ray said that he's often asked to name his favorite celebrity, but that "the secret to our show, the secret to our success, is being raised in a Christian home. We were taught to treat everybody with respect, and everybody equal. Every celebrity who attends our show gets the same treatment. They could be just a character actor. They could be a major star. They all get the same treatment." He slowed down to be sure I got this next part straight: "Our pastor has been out here twice. I'm sorry, he's been out here once. Our *associate* pastor has been out here twice. A couple of the deacons have been here. But our pastor wanted to meet Don Knotts. 'Cause he grew up watching *The Andy Griffith Show*, and he always wanted to meet Barney Fife. So, when he came out here, I actually made him Don's personal bodyguard for two days." Ray laughed so hard his voice cracked. "And he *loved* it! He loved it. And, so that's the secret to our success. Is to treat everybody with the same love and affection; and do not show any favoritism."

Sharon didn't think it was such a big deal to name her

somewhat mystifying favorite: "I could never believe Adriana Caselotti, the voice of Snow White, when she started comin' in."

Ray swiftly defused the appearance of favoritism: "Oh, what a sweetheart. And the voice of Cinderella, Ilene Woods."

Sharon stuck to her guns. "She was so funny, 'cause when she came in, she was sittin' at her table, and she would use her voice for me. And sing! And it just fascinated the kids—"

Ray clarified, "—now this is Snow White—"

And Sharon kicked off a round of back-and-forth, sentence-completing comments to give me the backstage scoop: "—and the other celebrities around her would tell Ray, they'd like to be moved somewhere else. You know, it's kinda—"

"—monotonous."

"You could hear it—"

"—all day long. All day long she's in character!"

"But she was a sweet person—"

"—until she died!" Ray gave a mournful little hoot. "Yeah, she done our show quite often."

"Quite often," Sharon said.

In the ballroom, death is on a lot of people's minds. Wayne Schulman, who works for a bond house, told me he started collecting autographs because, when Jack Benny died, he thought, "I'm never gonna get his autograph." Since then, he's amassed a huge collection, and for him, the Beverly Garland is a chance to "get them before they're dead." When I asked Darryl Bechthold, a video producer, what makes this show special for him, he said, "Several people have died since I started getting autographs here. Like Dr. Smith from . . . what's that TV series? Where they travel, with Guy Williams and the robot? Well, I just happened to get him and a picture, the time he was here before he died. I got him, and the next thing you know, he's gone. So you gotta get them now, or you're not going to get them."

I watched while Darryl bought a signed photo of Noel Neill, who played Lois Lane on TV's *Superman* with George Reeves in the 1950s. After Darryl paid her and left, I asked Noel if she was having fun. "Same old thing," she said. "Can't wait to get outta here."

She sounded serious, but I laughed as if she were joking: " 'Same old thing'? What does that mean?"

"People say they remember me. They liked *Superman.* That kind of thing." Her words clopped like hooves.

A man walked up and told the eighty-three-year-old, "You're America's sweetheart, you know that? Those old shows are just timeless, you know that?"

When he walked away, she rolled her eyes and said, "They grew up with me."

Larry Thomas Ward, her biographer (*Truth, Justice, & the American Way*, 2003), stepped in to soften her remark: "Noel's been around a long time. Noel's seen it all."

Later, Larry sent me a copy of Noel's biography, and I found out he was right. Since 1981, Noel has helped support herself by answering fan mail for Tom Selleck. In my files, I found signed pictures of both her and him that I'd received for free, by mail, when I was a kid. The handwriting on them is identical.

The money-changing that takes place at this show alters people. One veteran collector said, "A lot of celebrities get ruined by this. When you run into them on the outside, as civilians, they won't sign anymore once they do the Beverly Garland show. They get the Beverly Garland syndrome. One of my favorites who used to be an unbelievable signer was Shirley Jones. And the last couple of times I've seen her out, she says, 'Too busy.' When you get twenty dollars a pop, you know what you've got, and you won't give it away as easily."

Some fans are similarly changed at the bazaar. When Lorenzo Lamas charges $20 for signed pictures—and he's sitting right there doing it, and you watch him take your money—then you realize, *Lorenzo Lamas is worth $20*—and you might treat him accordingly. Felix Silla (Cousin Itt) said, "This to me is like the unemployment line. They all ask stupid questions. Look at my pictures and say, 'Which one is you?' Ha, ha. For me, this is just a chance to get out of the house. These fans, they're nice to you one minute, and then they'll walk right by and just ignore you."

Word got around that a reporter was at the show, and some of the more obscure stars eyed me pleadingly whenever I walked by. One, whom I couldn't bring myself to talk to, was Edwin "Hitchhiker" Neal from *The Texas Chainsaw Massacre*. He wore a T-shirt showing Mickey Mouse as the sorcerer's apprentice. Above his booth hung a movie poster, with this tagline:

Who Will Survive
And What
Will Be
Left Of
Them?

Erin Gray, of TV's *Buck Rogers in the 25th Century* and *Silver Spoons* told me, "Stars on a higher level wouldn't come here. It's personable because there is exchange. There's need on both sides." She said the stars at the Ramada "have interesting lives and we share. And guess what? We have a lot of opinions and ideas!" She talked about tai chi, as a metaphor for something. "They want to listen because I was Colonel Wilma Deering." Another actress, whom I did not recognize, whose name I did not write down because I did not think she was important, said, "I don't know which side of the cage I'm on."

There was no calliope, but a former *Playboy* Playmate had a boom box at her table, and she grooved in place to the Eurythmics' "Sweet Dreams." Nearby, Noel Neill glowered: "What is this, a *disco*?" Five hundred faces and bodies in the ballroom, air-conditioning on the fritz—Ray Courts flew by me, fanning sport-coat flaps: "Whoo-ee! B.O.!"—and I stepped outside for air, where a bank truck idled while the motel lobby's ATM was being refilled, and I was stunned to see a plump, white-maned old man perched on the edge of a brick planter, surrounded by fans, cheerfully signing autographs.

I asked Sharon Courts what Ray Bradbury was doing here. Was he going to sell his autograph at a table in the ballroom? Was he here to buy autographs from the ones inside?

She shrugged. "He usually shows up. He never gets a table. I think he just likes to hang around."

2

Little Soldiers

OUTSIDE THE COURTHOUSE IN Santa Ana, California, the screaming was so loud that Ben had to holler when he said, "This is as close as you're ever going to get to seeing Jesus." A minute later, Michael Jackson, who'd just been arraigned on charges of child molestation, hoisted himself onto the roof of his black SUV and started dancing, transporting fans to ecstasy: they were jumping, shaking, stretching out their arms, hoping what fans always hope when they get close to their idol—to be seen, to be a special person that stands out from the crowd.

Ben, the Beverly Hills–debeautifying autograph collector, had left that profession to become a paparazzi photographer, and he had been telling me for two years that Michael Jackson's connection with his fans was "the freakiest shit you've ever seen, 'cause it almost seems normal." Mike Wehrmann had called to tell me about them, too: "These girls, they follow him everywhere. They're smart and pretty and cool, and wherever he goes, they just sit outside for weeks, waiting. And they're not groupies. He's almost like buddies with them." Both Ben and Mike had sweetheart deals with Michael's fans, passing tips around when they heard about the singer's travel itinerary (e.g., Mike tells MJ fan where MJ's going to be; MJ fan pays back Mike by getting autographs for him). So

Ben hooked me up with a couple of key figures in this group, and I got to know a society of fans who are amateurs, in the best sense of the word. The professional-ization of fandom that I've been describing hasn't really sullied planet MJ—a place populated mostly by true believers.

With Daniela Kameke, a twenty-five-year-old university student who traveled from Berlin to be at the arraignment, I sprinted away from the bedlam and jumped in Ben's car. He tore down the road that Michael would be traveling, and we pulled over to watch the singer's vehicle approach. A sea of fans filled the street surrounding Michael's SUV, which crawled for a mile to keep from running people over. Policemen cleared the way, using billy clubs to beat back fans, who fell to the ground, clutching freshly bruised arms and legs, telling one another "I saw him!" and "He saw me!" When the way was clear for Michael's car to hit the highway, Ben raced back to Neverland, hitting one hundred miles an hour a couple seconds off the on-ramp. Midway there, he slammed on screeching brakes and swerved to keep from rear-ending a line of cars, then barked at me, "What? The *girl's* cool with this, and the *guy* is *screaming?*"

By a nose, we beat Michael to his own house, and Daniela waved him down at the gate of the estate. Through the open back window of the car, I saw Mi-chael's pale face floating in the dark interior, and Daniela jumped up on the running board, stuck her head inside, and said, "I love you and I support you. I come from Germany and there are many more from Germany who would have come but they could not afford it. They love you, too."

I couldn't hear Michael's response to her, and when I asked her what he'd said, she replied, " 'I love you, too, and something-something-something the media.' I couldn't hear it. He speaks so soft." Her breath was heavy and her skin was flushed. I asked if he had called her by name, and she said no, but that it didn't matter. "He saw me. He knew I was here. It made the whole trip worth it."

The night before, Lisadawn Marble, a thirty-year-old charity worker from Santa Rosa, had burst into a motel room in Solvang, California, where about a dozen of her fellow fans had spent the evening making posters and signs in support of the singer (YOU ARE A LEGEND / AND LEGENDS ARE INDESTRUCTIBLE). Brandishing a photo album, she asked, "Who wants to look at my pictures?" Someone raised a hand, and Lisadawn began to narrate the collection of snapshots in a rapid, high-pitched voice: "There's my bedspread. I have a Michael Jackson bedspread, chocolate bars, everything. In my apartment I have a Michael Jackson museum. It's my own private museum and I only let in the people I want to come . . . That's my life-sized statue of Michael, but it's bigger than life-sized. It's six feet four and he's five feet seven."

Michael Jackson's stature in the world outside Lisadawn's apartment had been declining, along with his record sales, for quite a while. Stories of his plastic surgeries, his unusual relationships with children, and the garish whimsy of his home at Neverland Ranch inspired widespread revulsion that, for many, was probably intensified by embarrassment for having once loved his music or his dancing.

Still, many thousands of fans remain unabashedly in thrall to Michael Jackson, and their dedication has only deepened as his personal troubles have grown. The president of his fan club, Deborah Dannelly, a forty-eight-year-old grandmother of two in Corpus Christi, Texas, told me that her Web site had ten million hits in the month preceding the arraignment. Since Michael's arrest, the club had gained about sixteen hundred new members—and lost only one. Though Deborah helped organize a weekend of fan events surrounding the arraignment, she couldn't be there. (She had to stay in Texas to take care of her father, who'd had a stroke on Christmas Day.) She promised me the gathering would attract "the biggest Michael fans in the world."

Predictably, the rally also attracted lots of opportunists: Michael Jackson impersonators, aspiring singers belting out spirituals ("This is great exposure," said one's manager), and fringe activists such as Najee Ali of Project Islamic Hope, who claimed that the rally was his idea and repeatedly said, "I'm not a Jackson fan. I'm a fan of justice." At one point, four reporters stood in line waiting their turn to interview the man in the Charlie Chaplin suit. And a number of African-Americans (many of whom rode to Santa Ana on "Caravan of Hope" buses donated by Jermaine Jackson) said they believed Michael was being treated unfairly because of his race. The largest portion of the crowd, though, were the sort of fans that Ben and Mike had described to me: middle-class white women under the age of thirty-five, a crew of longtime supporters from around the world with a highly specific attachment to the man they still honor as the King of Pop.

Pop music fandom, from Beatlemania to Madonna

wannabes, has usually been about rebellion and pleasure. In contrast, Michael Jackson fans describe their passion for the star as a moral duty. They see themselves as intermediaries to a holy innocent, representing what they perceive to be his values—generosity, humility, and love—in a world where goodness is persecuted.

Many describe their admiration for him as a kind of vocation. Jacqui Scott, a slender, stylish beauty consultant who flew in from England, said, "To be a fan is to see his goodness. I think some people, it's almost like they're chosen to see goodness in him. In history, [the majority of] people have always been scared of people who were good . . . Michael used to say, 'If it wasn't for the children of the world, I would throw in the towel.' When Michael was arrested, I understood what he meant. In a world where this can happen, if it wasn't for the innocents—the children and animals—there wouldn't be any hope."

For most, there was never any question of their coming to the rally. "He has given me so much, I just wanted him to see one more face in the crowd to support him in his being innocent," said a woman from Oregon, who skipped probation on a criminal offense that she declined to identify, to "be here for Michael."

Their attachment is not only to the singer, but also to their fellow fans. They are in constant touch via instant messages and on Internet message boards, where they organize local social gatherings and vigils. A student from the University of Louisiana at Lafayette said he was too embarrassed to tell his college friends where he was going that weekend. "I say I have a family gathering. But this *is* a family gathering. These are the people who are there for you."

A jolly woman from Texas interrupted with an earnest explanation that gradually crescendoed to a rallying cry: "This is my brother, this is my sister. That's what Michael pretty much teaches. And I pump everybody up. I say, 'You don't have to be *ashamed* to be a fan.'"

Emboldened by her call, other fans responded: "He's like a father or brother or uncle to me."

"He's not Jesus Christ or anything. But he is an angel."

"His music has saved people from suicide."

They were unanimous in believing that Michael was innocent of the crimes with which he had been charged. Diana D'Alo, a thirty-year-old Italian fan who works for a French film-distribution company in Santa Monica, made a general defense of his goodness ("Michael loves children. He would never hurt a child") supported by personal observation ("I was at Neverland with Michael and the boy that's accusing him after the things were supposed to have taken place. And everything was normal. Nothing seemed wrong").

The fans don't exactly embrace Michael Jackson's eccentricities; they simply deny that he's strange. A sixteen-year-old from Gilroy, California, thought it was fine for Michael Jackson to share his bed with prepubescent boys: "If a child loves you, they want to have everything to do with you, even sleep with you. I know that from babysitting." When I asked fan club president Deborah Dannelly if she was troubled by the news clips of Michael Jackson dangling his baby from a high balcony at a Berlin hotel, I got an earful of jesuitical precision: "*Dangle*, if you look it up in the dictionary, means 'to hold out for an extended period of time.' That was a second and a half. I timed it.

That is not a dangle. I'm not saying that it was the smartest thing or the right thing to do. But it wasn't so different from any of us throwing our babies up and catching them in our arms."

Most surprising, though, were their responses when asked about his plastic surgeries. Many fans, like Micah Campbell, a twenty-three-year-old grocery store manager from Baxley, Georgia, believe the press has exaggerated the singer's transformation: "Sure, he doesn't look the same as he did twenty years ago. But you don't, I don't. Nobody does." Many more fans called his transformation insignificant. "It is not the appearance of a person that makes them who they are," said Deborah Dannelly. "If there's one person that's taught us that, it's Michael. If Michael or anybody chooses to change their appearance, it doesn't make him a different person. The fans don't see that as an issue."

Fans pooh-pooh the plastic surgeries because they believe they know the "real" Michael, a character whose essence has not changed since he sang "ABC" with the Jackson Five. The more the media points to Michael Jackson's nose as proof that he's gone off the deep end, the more entrenched grow the fans' belief that he hasn't really changed at all. This seems even more amazing when you consider that they have been the most avid consumers of Michael's image through the many stages of the metamorphosis that they deny or discount.

Maybe, I suggested to one fan, she couldn't see the changes precisely because she had been watching her idol so closely: "Maybe it's like seeing your own face in the mirror?"

No, she said, I didn't understand at all. "The press sees

what it wants to see. Michael fans see the actual person underneath."

At first I thought her claim of special knowledge was just a moony adolescent fantasy. I heard so many versions of this remark from so many fans that for a long time, I couldn't hear its texture. Now I think that it's the key to understanding the moral dimension of their devotion, the pleasure they derive from defending him, and the way that pleasure helps define their own identities.

The world maintains a morbid interest in Michael Jackson because he seems to have ceased to be an "actual person" such as the fans claim to know. Psychobabble about the singer's lost childhood can only superficially account for his eccentricities; beyond that, the man appears to be pure entropy. It is impossible to imagine his peculiarities and alleged crimes adding up to anything coherent enough to be called character. That makes him a magnet for the media, who rush into the blankness and build a monster for the rest of us to cringe at.

As Michael Jackson's public story grows more gruesome, his fans believe they have a moral duty to assert his essential goodness all the more. Their righteous pleasure in defending him is compounded by a sense of exclusivity: the world may see them as fools, but they know they are the faithful remnant.

The fans' claims to know Michael's secret self are, at the same time, and perhaps more fundamentally, claims to have secret selves of their own. I think that's what they tried to tell me, and why they seemed so satisfied by pushing me away every time they said, "You can't understand me." To be a Michael Jackson fan is to be someone special: a person so extraordinary that you cannot be explained—and at the same time, so unusual as to command outsiders' attention.

The queen of the fans is probably Diana D'Alo, a voluptuous brunette whose blue eyes are often shaded by Chanel sunglasses that she keeps in a Gucci purse, and who sometimes appears at Jackson family press conferences to represent the fans' perspective. When Michael is in trouble, she is in such demand for media interviews that giving them is practically "another full-time job." She says she hates being interviewed because reporters always get things wrong, but she consents because "Michael needs the world to know the truth."

Her one-bedroom apartment in Santa Monica is simply and sparsely furnished, and the only photograph I saw displayed there was a small color snapshot of her riding a bus with Michael. She looks straight into the camera; he appears in profile, gazing out the window, the details of his face dissolving into glaring light.

Diana first saw Michael Jackson's photograph on a magazine cover at a newsstand in Italy when she was fifteen. It stopped her cold. "I had never seen a person like that before. He looked so strange and beautiful." Recalling the moment, she paused before each adjective, savoring her own words as if they were food.

She passed through an early phase of teenybopper infatuation and memorabilia collecting, and then, when she began to meet the singer with some frequency about ten years ago, sold her collection to other fans so she could travel to see his concerts. Their first meeting, at her tenth concert (in Madrid), took place when she rushed the stage while he sang "She's Out of My Life."

"I had seen him before, but he hadn't seen me. That was the first time he really saw me," she explained. She said they chatted briefly, but when I asked her to describe the exchange, she shot me a slightly pitying look: "That is personal. That is just for me."

No other celebrity has ever exerted such a pull on her, and when I asked why she cares so much for Michael, she answered with two questions of her own: "How do you explain emotion? How do you explain love?"

Diana took me under her wing for the weekend, and I was grateful for her protection. The Michael Jackson message boards I'd been perusing on the Web roiled with warnings against talking to reporters: *they will TWIST EVERY LITTLE THING U SAY and MAKE U LOOK LIKE A FANATIC instead of a REAL TRUE PERSON who LOVES Michael Jackson! they only care about THEM-SELVES, THE LIES THEY MAKE UP, and THE NEXT BIG STORY! that's what happens when you sell your soul to the DEVIL.* (This gives a flavor of the caution; legal restrictions on the message board contents prevent direct quotation.)

Most fans began their conversations with me with a defensive insult ("You just want to say I'm crazy") or a plea ("Please, just please don't make me look stupid"). Diana, who was convinced by our first meeting (and, more crucially, by Ben's endorsement) that I probably wasn't out to get her, agreed to help me get past their defenses by introducing me around.

She told me I could follow her in my car to the weekend's first fan gathering, a rally at the Santa Barbara courthouse. She did not tell me that her cruising speed was ninety. When we arrived, she strode serenely toward a noisy gathering of about sixty fans, who were surrounded by about eighty members of the press. Before plunging in, she paused to apply some lip gloss and scan the scene.

"Ah," she said coolly, "the French," and nodded to a couple of fiercely elegant, bone-skinny, chain-smoking women in white T-shirts standing at opposite ends of a ratty French flag on whose bands of color they had sloppily written a few slogans. Blue implored the reader, "Before you judge him, try hard to love him." White laid out the creed of reasons that one ought to try: "Michael Jackson is / Achieved Dream / A caring heart / A new vision / A lesson of life / Hope for Tomorrow / A Philosophy / A Concept of Love." Red wrapped things up with a disillusioned yelp: "When Michael Jackson is being arrested, you know the world has gone crazy."

Diana cocked one impeccably plucked eyebrow and said, "They are a little strange." When I asked why, she wrinkled her nose at their crude banner and sniffed, "If you are going to do a thing, you do it right."

Then she exclaimed, "The Spanish!" and waved to a group of petite, dark-haired women dressed in Billabong jerseys and sexy scoop-necked, striped blouses rocking out on the courthouse steps with a boom box that played "Tabloid Junkie," Michael Jackson's jeremiad against the media from the *HIStory* album. We made our way through an asteroid belt of cameramen and reporters and entered the mass of fans who were dancing and singing, and Diana's lips began to move in sync with the whole crowd's:

"Just because you read it in a magazine / Or see it on the TV screen don't make it factual."

One of the Spanish nudged another and said, "This—what we are doing—is what the lyrics are about. This is what this song is *for*."

A playlist of angry anthems chronicling the singer's fury at the press and the police continued with "Scream," "They Don't Care About Us" ("Beat me, bash me / You can never trash me"), and repeatedly—and with the greatest satisfaction—"D.S.," a vilifying screed against a person identified in the lyrics as "Dom Sheldon." When sung, the name sounds like "Tom Sneddon," the Santa Barbara district attorney who is Michael's legal nemesis. "You think he brother with the KKK? . . . / Dom Sheldon is a cold man . . ."

The French, the Spanish, the Norwegians, the Swedish, the Japanese, the English, and the rest—almost all of them with smiles on their faces—danced and sang until somehow there emerged consensus that it was time to check in at their motels (where they would get ready for the candlelight vigil outside Neverland that preceded the poster-making sessions, which lasted so long that plans for a group expedition to a local multiplex, where *Peter Pan* was playing, had to be scrapped).

Diana kept busy racing around greeting everyone, and talking to a few reporters. She would check in on me every so often, each time raising her voice above the angry songs to ask some version of the same question: "It is fun, yes?"

The next morning I arrived at the Santa Ana courthouse well before the sun came up. It was freezing in the dark, but Diana had dressed warmly. "Yes," she said, "leather pants are warm."

Though she was unlucky in the lottery for seats to watch the arraignment in the courtroom that morning, Diana was determined to find a way in. I followed her, high-stepping inconspicuously across the wires and cables that snaked among the TV satellite trucks alongside the courthouse, and falling into line with the lottery winners as they prepared to enter the building. Diana made the most of her eyelashes when it came time to sweet-talk the guards who asked for our tickets.

Though rebuffed, she was not the least bit angry or hostile. When I opened my mouth to ask a question, she laid her hand on my shoulder: "Let me think. There must be some way." This challenge seemed small-time to Diana, who has crashed the Romanian parliament, pretty much every major concert venue in the world, and "a dentist's office in Mexico" in order to see Michael. We poked around and tried some doors, all of which were locked. I thought she might get frustrated after a while, but after exhausting all visible options of entry, she said, "Don't you have fun with me?" and I laughed. I actually did.

We ducked into a building behind the courthouse to warm up, and Diana asked, "I am maybe not so crazy as you thought?"

Well, I said, what we were doing was a little odd, and illegal, but it was still fun.

She clutched the collar of her fur-lined toggle coat and pressed for reassurance: "So we are not crazy."

"No," I said. "I do think you are a little crazy. I think that all the best parts of us—all of our talents, and all of our enthusiasms—they're always partly sane, and they're always partly crazy. Don't you?"

Warily she said, "Okay," broke eye contact for a moment, and then surprised me with a sudden confidence: "The fans, many of them come from broken homes. Many have lost a parent. Many of the girls have eating disorders. Yes, with all of them following Michael around, they are trying to fill up some lack. But that is true of everybody, with what they are enthusiastic about."

I tried to take advantage of the opening: "For you, what is the lack?"

She shook her head and chuckled. "No, no. That is not what I am going to talk about."

Pushing, I got nowhere, and finally I said, "Even if you won't tell me what it is, do you know what lack you're trying to fill?"

"I am not sure," she said, and I couldn't tell whether she meant it, so I just kept looking at her until she talked some more. "Another thing about all Michael fans is that they're childlike. Look at us. We're thirty years old. And the way we're dressed, the way we act, how old would you think we are? At least ten years younger. We're people who don't want our childhood to end. But I can't psychoanalyze Michael Jackson fans for you." Her expression went opaque: that was enough of that.

"I should go back," she said, meaning back to the front of the courthouse. "The TV people, I think they need fans to interview."

"Diana, sometimes I think you like being interviewed."

"Oh, no"—she hid all but a shadow of a smile—"I only do it for Michael."

*   *   *

Diana is a central figure in a core group of several dozen Michael Jackson fans whose lives are largely ordered by their desire to see the singer in person at every possible opportunity. Most of these fans are unusually attractive, fashionably dressed, and well-spoken European women over twenty-one and under forty who refer to themselves as "girls." Dulce Iglesias, a twenty-nine-year-old Spanish fan who helps run a family-owned restaurant in London, estimated that in the previous year she had taken eight "Michael trips," lasting "anywhere from five days to a month." The women often travel in packs of four to six, usually with others from their home countries. Sometimes they follow the singer's concert tours; sometimes they simply wait outside the gates of Neverland Ranch for weeks at a time, in hopes that he will notice them on his way in or out of the property.

Stuart Backerman, Michael's former publicist who served as a liaison to the fans, explained the phenomenon to me this way: "They're not sitting outside of Neverland for three weeks because he's a great singer. They're sitting there because he's a great person, with a message—that we should erase the color lines, that we should look at people not for what they are outwardly, but for what they are inwardly, and that if we do that together, we can heal the world—that all of us need to hear." This is an exaggeration, but it is not just talk. Many of the fans I met do volunteer work for children's charities as a way of showing their devotion to Michael.

Quite a few of them have been following him for a decade or more, and he rewards and stokes their loyalty. Bea Arizna, twenty-four, who owns a nightclub in Oviedo, Spain, said, "If we are standing outside his hotel or his house, he will always come out. He recognizes us and says, 'Are you okay? Why are you here?' " He has never insulted them, the way the Rolling Stones, Bob Dylan, Madonna, and many other performers have at times snubbed and offended their admirers.

This unwavering generosity helps to explain why the fans' feelings for him seem to be entirely affirmative: what they describe as their "love" for Michael Jackson strikingly (and, in my experience with fans, almost uniquely) has no apparent undertones of hate. He sometimes invites them to have supper or watch movies with him at Neverland, although they declined to discuss these experiences in detail because they sign nondisclosure agreements upon entering the house. "I love the popcorn at Neverland," said Daniela Kameke. "It tastes better than any popcorn in the world." When some fans who attended Michael's Madison Square Garden concerts on September 7 and 10, 2001, were stranded in New York when air traffic halted after 9/11, Michael assigned them a bodyguard, paid for several of them to stay in the Helmsley Palace Hotel, chartered a bus to take them shopping, and covered all of their expenses until they could return home. "The Spanish embassy said they couldn't help me," Dulce remembered, "but Michael did."

Usually, though, their devotion doesn't come cheap. Some have run up massive credit card bills. Jacqui Scott said, "My family worries because of the debt. But they know that I just need to see Michael at times." Daniela Kameke, shivering slightly in a thin wool coat, said that she works "several jobs" to afford her trips. "I don't spend any money on anything anymore. No clothes. I never go

out. Every single Euro I spend, I think, 'I could spend it on the trips.' It's only on Christmas or birthdays that I get new clothes."

The sacrifices they make for Michael's sake are not just financial. They are also emotional. At the courthouse rally, Jacqui Scott expressed some bewilderment at the persistence of her ardor: "Some people let go of the things that helped them through their childhood. With Michael, it's kind of like he's this lost child. And a lot of his fans are like lost children. Please don't make me sound crazy. Because I am not crazy. I am trusting you. I have been like this since I was twelve."

Jacqui said she was the only black girl in the English village where she grew up. She was teased and put down by other children. "I hated my childhood. But as a child, I always felt that Michael loved me. You feel someone like that can never hurt you, because you're never close with them. So you can never be hurt by them. You go to people who can't hurt you."

She followed the entire *Bad* tour, the *Dangerous* tour, and "ninety percent of the *HIStory* tour." She said that she has met Michael "dozens of times. He's only said my name once. It was in New York the year before last, at a Democratic Party fund-raiser. I think he's one of the nicest people I've ever met."

I was having trouble understanding: "He's only said your name once. You're not friends. You know that. And yet you're telling me that he is one of the nicest people you've ever met. What am I missing?"

"It sounds weird, but it's spiritual." She paused to scowl at a fundamentalist Christian doing some bullhorn evangelism: "Quit being deceived by this phony celebrity stuff!

If you get cancer tomorrow, who's gonna be there for you? Is Michael Jackson gonna be there for you?"

"I was just drawn to him, from when I very first saw a video. A few weeks after that, I'm like I am now, and I've been like that for more than twenty years."

Her interest in Michael Jackson, like most of these fans', is almost completely nonsexual. When they occasionally allow that he's "hot," the adjective is uttered with blushing and embarrassment. It's a curious discomfort. Sex appeal is usually a core element of pop fandom: admirers of Elvis and the Beatles, for instance, viewed their idols as objects of sexual fantasy or as models of sexual liberation. The majority of Michael Jackson fans I talked with, by contrast, seemed embarrassed about sex, perhaps because Michael's own sexuality appears to be so confused.

More likely, their embarrassment has little to do with Michael. The first thing you notice about most of these women is their beauty. Ben said, "It's not like fans of other rock stars. Go to a U2 concert, and they're all butt ugly. These girls are *hot*. They could have boyfriends in a second, if they wanted." Beauty takes work, and these women clearly devote considerable time and resources to looking their best; but almost all of them are unable to take compliments on their appearance. Most of them are also single, and sensitive about the topic: "That is a personal question. That has nothing to do with anything. Why would you ask about that?" said Daniela Kameke when I asked if she had a boyfriend. She had been friendly until then, and she barely talked to me afterward. Their own sexuality was the only topic, aside from media misrepresentation of Michael Jackson, that seemed to upset these fans.

(I have run across only one other fan group that is so notably asexual. The television series *Beauty and the Beast* has a large following among people who have been physically disfigured, and those who have been victims of sexual abuse. These fans idealize the purity of the love affair between the show's main characters—a love that is passionate but can never be sexual. None of the Michael Jackson fans made any comments to me indicating that they were victims of sexual abuse. Still, I couldn't help but wonder about parallels to *Beauty and the Beast*. Quite possibly, people who have been abused and have chosen never to reveal it might be drawn to idealize a man who symbolizes childhood innocence and absolute goodness. The attachment of such people to such a character might be forcefully asexual and avowedly pure; and they would jump to his defense if he were accused of the kind of crimes that they would prefer not to confront.)

Though they say their interest in Michael isn't romantic, a number of these fans do share at least one habit with love-struck schoolgirls: they regularly write letters to Michael, which they hand-deliver at his public appearances in distinctively designed envelopes. Myra Juliette, a poised, raven-haired twenty-nine-year-old from Amsterdam, described the envelopes as "insurance that he'll know you." Her envelope bears a black-and-white line drawing of a child holding a ball of fire in his hands; another woman's bears three identical images of Charlie Chaplin's body with Michael's face.

When I asked the woman with the Charlie Chaplin envelope (she refused to give her name, for fear that colleagues at her fancy European media job would disapprove) if Michael ever wrote her back, she said, "No, and I don't expect him to. I don't write to get an answer. I write so that I can give him encouragement and praise."

Myra is committed to a constant search for moments of personal contact with Michael Jackson, but she, like the other fans I've described, does not seem to suffer any delusion of personal closeness to the singer. "Being a fan is completely different from the world that Michael is in," Myra said. "But you're part of something special. We see Michael the way he is."

The inner circle of Michael Jackson fans are willing to accept a relationship that is less than intimate at the center of their lives because of the sense of adventure that it provides—and the special knowledge of his true self, or of their own selves, that it seems to impart. I wanted to know, as precisely as I could, what part of themselves these fans were defending, by defending Michael Jackson. They dismissed that kind of question because they rejected its premise. Pop psychology is so often used as a weapon for discrediting their happiness that they've trained themselves not to think or talk about the psychological roots of their fascination.

Hanging out with these fans, I felt like I was in a time warp. I hadn't listened to Michael's music since I was a kid because I'd been put off by his bizarre publicity. But when I spent time with the fans, I started revisiting his greatest hits, and I remembered the thrill of hearing these songs for the first time. Michael Jackson was to the early eighties what the Beatles were to the early sixties: a sound and style that seemed entirely new, and ours.

At a candlelight vigil the night before the arraignment,

standing in the driveway of Neverland, I asked Myra, what causes one fan to leave her sequined glove in a drawer, with other outgrown mementos, and another to leave home to follow him around the world?

Down the road, a car stereo was playing songs from 1983, and Michael Jackson's high-pitched cries and crowing filled the pauses as she answered, "Maybe there are two people who love dancing. Maybe one of those two people becomes a professional dancer, and the other doesn't. Maybe they both have the same amount of talent, and all the same choices, but maybe one person prefers to follow their dream and the other prefers to accept that they're a great dancer, and that's it. Maybe we're the people who followed our dream.

"I've been to places most people will never go," she said. "Estonia, Korea. Because of Michael, I have friends in Angola. I could go to Japan and I have twenty friends there. I've been on the floor of parliament in Romania. And Britain. And yet, in the end, he's a stranger to me."

Lights from the television stand-up crews behind her flashed on and off, and the features of her face flashed from detail to silhouette. "But if it makes me happy, why not follow him? Years from now, think of the stories I'll have to tell."

At the end of J. M. Barrie's *Peter Pan*, Wendy, Michael, John, and the lost boys return from Neverland to the real world. When the boys grow up, the narrator makes the melancholy judgment that "it is scarcely worth while saying anything more about them. You may see the twins Nibs and Curly any day going to an office, each carrying a little bag and umbrella . . . The bearded man who doesn't know any story to tell his children was once John."

Sometimes I have a strong urge to wish little bags and umbrellas and offices on Michael Jackson's lost girls. Years from now, Myra may have great stories to tell. And yet, if she and Diana and Dulce and Bea and Jacqui and the rest never stop flying around the world chasing Michael Jackson, who will they have to tell their stories to? It's an important question, but the more I think about it, the less I understand the point of asking it. Someday, many of the rest of us, with our jobs and marriages and mortgages, may begin to wish we could see Estonia or Angola or Japan. We'll probably wait until we're seventy to start our trips around the world, at which point we might decide that Cancún would be a little easier, because who knows when that hip might go out again? Enchantment keeps its own hours.

After the arraignment, Michael Jackson threw a party at Neverland. The line of cars to get into the ranch was more than two miles long. At the gate, some of the fans asked me to come inside with them. I told them I couldn't because reporters were barred unless we agreed to sign a nondisclosure agreement that forbade us to describe anything we saw there.

"But you owe it to yourself. There is no place like Neverland," Dulce said.

"Just stop being a reporter for a while," Diana said. "You would have so much fun."

I told them I was going to sit this one out. If I went to Neverland, I wouldn't be doing my job, and I was there to do a job. I stayed outside the gate watching fans stream in until I got bored. I drove to my motel, where I watched TV until I got restless, and got back in my car and drove again to the ranch. I remembered what Daniela had said about the popcorn, and thought about how much I like Ferris wheels. Why was I scrupling? This could be Michael Jackson's last hurrah, and I was missing it because I feared my integrity would be marred by what would be, in the scheme of things, a trivial compromise that might bring me a lot of pleasure? I caught sight of a reporter I knew inside the estate and wondered if the rules about press coverage had changed, or if I had misunderstood.

I began to think that I would regret it for the rest of my life if I did not see the inside of Neverland. So I started making phone calls, pretty frantically, trying to find someone who could get me into the party, but to no avail.

After the party was over, I stopped by the motel room where the Spanish women were staying, where Diana and Daniela were also hanging out. They were all flung across the bedspreads, eating pizza and cheese curls and drinking Pepsi, watching the day's news on TV. Switching channels, they came upon a rerun of a documentary about Michael Jackson. "This is when we were in Las Vegas waiting for Michael for a month!" one said.

On-screen, Michael was shopping in a tacky Las Vegas store, buying thousands of dollars' worth of enameled, gilt, and ormolu vases, clocks, and knickknacks. Wide-eyed, Dulce turned to me and said, "Everything in Neverland is like that, all bright colors and gold."

Tentatively Diana said, "Today I didn't like it, for the first time."

"What?" another woman asked, still looking at the

TV—and suddenly the Spanish were all talking over one another, furious over some lapse of continuity in the show. The scene shifted to a sidewalk in Vegas, and two of the women in the motel room appeared on-screen. Michael gestured to them and softly told the documentary's host, "The Spanish fans are so sweet. They're beautiful people. Stunning to look at."

In the motel room, they giggled and repeated his words to one another, and Dulce turned back to Diana: "What were you saying?"

Diana said, "Nothing." Then: "I was looking around the house for two hours. I was looking at all the details. And it all seemed so tacky. It was weird. I didn't like it."

No one answered her. The scene had shifted again and some of the women were recognizing themselves among a crowd sprinting down a street in Berlin. They pointed fingers at blurry figures on the screen and someone cried out, "That's me in the green coat!"

"That's me running!"

"This is me!"

If there is an anti–Michael Jackson, it might be Dolly Parton. Where he is a singular American tragedy, she is a rousing American success story. His life is a warning: if you radically transform yourself, you may lose yourself completely, and the world will revile you. Her life is an inspiration: by transforming, you can become more essentially yourself, and everyone will love you for it.

Still, the two inspire devotion that's quite similar. Fans of every entertainer believe they have special knowledge of their stars, but none I've met state this belief so assuredly as

Dolly's and Michael's. Initially I found these claims confounding because they refer to such synthetic human beings. Dolly, who has said, "I look at myself like a show horse," and who sometimes refers to her "fixed-up" breasts as "little soldiers," is just as open about her surgeries as Michael is secretive about his. Her candor makes her a paradox of artifice and authenticity: no star is more fake, and no star is more real.

For fans of both, the ultimate expression of commitment is a pilgrimage, a visit to their star's amusement park. There's one big difference between these destinations, reflecting the contrast of their characters. Neverland is also Michael's home, a private place where entry is by invitation only; and Dollywood (in her hometown of Pigeon Forge, Tennessee) is a business, a public place that's open to anyone who can afford a ticket. Consequently, Michael's fans can't complete their journey unless he becomes involved with them, choosing them to come inside. Dolly's fans make pilgrimage on their own steam.

This difference also complicates the contrast. Michael, the more reclusive, is more personally available to fans; and Dolly, though more open, is less accessible. A sixteen-year-old fan told me that when she met Michael Jackson, "He said, 'I love you,' to me. I almost died. He tried to find a way to hold my hand, but he couldn't because my hand was clenched so tight. I could feel his nails struggling to find a way to open my hand so he could hold it." If Dolly tried to do that, her nails could snap right off.

I went to Neverland as a curiosity seeker, mystified by the ardor of the people I would meet. I went to Dollywood as one of the faithful, a fan with something to be thankful for.

When I was in grade school, Dolly Parton was a joke: the name we used to tease the girls whom puberty hit hardest. For a while, in the *Nine to Five* era, she was cool. I'd sing along to that movie's theme song, imagining I identified with her suffering and striving, although I had no idea that "pour myself a cup of ambition" meant coffee. She came back into my life when I came out, when I heard her dance version of "Peace Train" at a club one night and her voice called me like a prophet: "Come and join the living / It's not so far from you . . ."

A few years after that, I heard her gospel song "I Am Ready," and its lyrics—the deathbed speech of an old woman who asks her children to read to her from her Bible before she goes—just about undid me. Not long before, my family had put my mother, who had been disappearing into Alzheimer's disease for years, into a nursing home. Before hearing Dolly's song, I hadn't thought to wonder what it might be like for my mom to face death without anyone reading to her from the Bible, the book she used to make sense of life's ultimate questions and to reassure herself that, no matter how bad things seemed to be, God would finally make everything all right. Listening to "I Am Ready" again and again, the song became a kind of tool for me, chipping at the edges of inarticulate fears and feelings that I had been avoiding, and helping me to understand that there are things you have to do for people and things you have to tell them before they die, or else those things will never be done and said.

The next time I went home to Illinois, I took Mom's Bible to the nursing home. She barely even focused her eyes anymore, and she had lost the ability to converse, but I spent a long time talking to her. I finally told her that I'm gay, something I'd kept secret because I had figured it out around the time that she'd received her diagnosis, and I had worried that the news would be too upsetting or confusing for her. But when I told her, she focused her eyes and smiled at me. I described Dolly's song and what it had made me realize; I said that I was sorry that I hadn't thought to make sure somebody was reading the Bible to her. Then I read to her from Revelation, where God makes a new heaven and a new earth, and there is no more suffering. It was the last time I saw her before she died.

If I hadn't heard "I Am Ready," something else would probably have brought me to the same realizations and prodded me to do the same things. But that's not the way it happened. I had my last true connection with my mom because of Dolly Parton. Or, that's how I understood it, until I went to Dollywood.

The winding, wooded road to Dollywood is lined with welcome signs, all bearing pictures of butterflies. The butterfly of Dollywood's logo is not delicate or pretty. It's lumpen, with splashy red, magenta, purple, and blue spots on gold wings, heavily outlined in black. The outline distorts the illustration's scale in such a way that, if the image were transformed into an actual butterfly, its wings would be about as thick as pats of butter.

Inside the amusement park, this butterfly is plastered on practically every surface that will take paint, down to the shot glasses in the gift shop (called the Butterfly Emporium). It's the perfect logo for the park because the story of the butterfly is Dolly Parton's story. Like the crawling caterpillar that becomes a soaring burst of color, Dolly started life as a poor girl in the Smoky Mountains and became a glamorous star.

Her work records this metamorphosis. Gary Wade, a Tennessee judge who went to high school with Dolly, told me that his family owned a store where the Parton family often traded: "We had samples of suits, and my mother gave them to Mrs. Parton thinking that she would use them some way, maybe on a quilt. The colors of the rags were black and brown and gray, maybe an off-white. Not red and blue and yellow. Not the colors of the rainbow. Mrs. Parton came in the store one day and showed the coat she made out of them. It was sort of drab. When you turn that memory into a song, you turn those muted colors bright. Dolly saw it as a 'Coat of Many Colors.' "

In her memoir, *My Life and Other Unfinished Business* (1994), Dolly tells a story about chasing a monarch butterfly when she was a child:

> I would get as close as I could to it and hold my hand up to where I could feel the breeze from its wings, but I was careful not to touch it. I knew that holding it would make the color come off of its wings like powder on my hands and that if I did that, the butterfly wouldn't be able to fly anymore. I used to imagine it was some kind of magic powder that gave them the power to fly. Maybe if I had enough of it to rub on me, I could fly too. But that would mean hurting an awful lot of butterflies, and I wanted them to fly. I'd just have to watch and fly with him in spirit.

One could read this as a veiled warning to fans, a parable to teach the risks of drawing too close to creatures that look magical. During my visit to Pigeon Forge, an English scientist announced a discovery that yields a related caution. By putting butterflies in a wind tunnel, this scientist found that their wing beats are nowhere near as simple as they look. If you or I walked down the street the way a butterfly moves through the air, we would get nowhere by just putting one foot in front of another. We would have to leap and skip and hop on one leg. We would backflip, somersault, and cartwheel, without even giving it a thought.

Entering Chasing Rainbows, the museum at Dollywood devoted to Dolly Parton's life history, I was greeted at the door by Thomasina Bicer. "Hi there! Would you like a rainbow?" She patted a rainbow sticker on my lapel and smiled: "Now you can chase your dreams, just like Dolly."

Dollywood means the world to Thomasina. Nine years earlier, when she first visited the park on a vacation from her home in Williamstown, New Jersey, she found a "peace haven" that changed her life. "I was on five different medications for high blood pressure and depression, and after I got back from here and listened to her records I went off them completely. Doctors asked me what happened, and I said, 'Dolly did that to me.'" Thomasina visited the park six or seven times a year for the next seven years, then moved to east Tennessee and began working at the park.

"After I moved here, I wrote her a thank-you note. I said that she was an angel to me. I told her I feel that she saved my life. If it wasn't for her making a peaceful, loving, godly place to calm me, I would have gotten sicker." She mailed the letter but received no response.

"It's okay," Thomasina said without resentment. "She's a very busy person."

Thomasina's experience is not unique. Many people who love Dolly Parton believe they have a special relationship with the star. They believe Dolly cares for them personally, and yet they say they are so secure in her affections that if she's too busy chasing rainbows to reciprocate in conventional ways, that's just fine.

Stephen Powers, a deaf man who is working on a doctorate in creative writing at the University of Wisconsin, Milwaukee, sent me a poem called "Chasing Parades," which describes the particular, vertiginous kind of intimacy that Dolly's fans experience. It begins, "I wear the red and blue fuzzy orchid shirt so she'll see me. / It flaps around me when I dance up and down, wave my arms over my head, / holler *Hi Dolly Hi Dolly* until she winks, motions back." After this moment of connection comes a reality check: "When the parade's over / they roll her away faster than your last dime / under a soda machine." And yet, the poem's final stanza speculates, "Dolly's probably in her dressing room or back in Nashville. / She says to her husband *Did you see that deaf guy's shirt this year?* / She fluffs her wig on its Styrofoam head, unlocks her real curls, rubs off some / eyeshadow, pulls the belt of her silk blue cotton candy robe tighter."

Dollywood, like Dolly herself, is a paradoxical creation. In her autobiography, Dolly described the park as an expression of wild ambition: the first time she visited Los Angeles, she looked up at the Hollywood sign and thought, "I would like to change that 'H' into a 'D.'" At the same time, she described it as an offering of pure-hearted altruism: "The theme park is much more about the mountains and the culture of the people who live there than it is about Dolly Parton . . . I saw Dollywood as a chance to honor them."

Perhaps most important, she also wanted the park to induce the feeling that she had had when she'd visited a carnival sideshow as a girl. Venturing inside a tent that held the "Alligator Girl from the Nile," she felt "a combination of hope that the thing could be true and fear that the thing could be true that is the very definition of mystery." What Dolly found inside that tent would have disillusioned many people. The Alligator Girl, a woman in a swimsuit with scales of green-dyed cornflakes glued to her skin, was her long-lost cousin. " 'Hey, Myrtle, it's me, Dolly,' I said, tapping on the glass."

At this discovery, Dolly's wonder only grew. "I could understand Myrtle completely. After all, I wanted to leave the mountains, too, and I wanted attention. She probably thought I was making fun or blowing her cover, but I just wanted to say, 'Hello, I understand. Be the alligator girl. Be whatever your dreams and your luck will let you be. Wear your green cornflakes with pride . . . Give them a quarter's worth of wonder.' "

Dollywood does evoke this kind of wonder, especially inside Chasing Rainbows, whose runic exhibits begin with a narrow, low-ceilinged, dimly lit passage showing mementos of the childhood she's mythologized in song (a brightened re-creation of the "coat of many colors," the medicine bag of "Dr. Robert F. Thomas," who was present for her birth). As her career begins, the galleries broaden and lighten, and the visitor is invited to ascend by Dolly's side. Stand in front of a blue screen and watch yourself on a video monitor, singing a duet of "Together Always" with a youthful Dolly: "Forever and ever / Together always, you and me." When she becomes a superstar, the path through the museum leads down a dazzling atrium, where her flashy dresses—sewn with sequins big as cornflakes—are all on show; and once you've seen them, at the moment when you're ready for a rest, you'll spy a row of stools off to one side, each facing a small TV screen on which floats the image of one of Dolly's golden wigs. Take a seat, and watch your face appear on-screen, crowned by Dolly's hairdo—and in that giddy moment, you will feel both hope and fear that this image of yourself could be somehow true. What would it be like to chase your dreams, just like Dolly?

Unlike Michael's fans, who revel in the exclusivity of their connection with the singer, Dolly's fans love the universality of her appeal. Thomasina dilated, "There is not one person in this world that can say they don't like Dolly. People are crazy if they can't find one thing about her to identify with, that makes them want to follow their dreams the way she did."

Dolly's fans do share with Michael's a belief that their devotion calls them to improve the world. Dolly has encouraged this idea: she disbanded her fan club in 1997 and asked its members to send their money to her favorite charities instead. Two fans who've taken seriously her call to give are Patric Parkey and Harrell Gabehart, both in their forties, of Irving, Texas. Each year they attend charity auctions endorsed by Dolly, where they bid on memorabilia to add to the collection that fills their four-teen-hundred-square-foot home—"every room, floor to ceiling, wall to wall," Patric said. Among their greatest treasures: one of Dolly's license plates, one of her wigs, and a Dolly Parton pinball machine. When I met them, they were considering moving their bedroom into the garage to make room for more.

Having photos of the star all over their house, Harrell told me, "brings out the best in both of us. It's kind of hard to look at her all the time and not get closer to one another, because she teaches about family values and being supportive of one another." Like Thomasina, Harrell has struggled with depression, and he finds that Dolly's music helps to keep him well. "When you believe in what she says, it's hard to stay depressed." Patric and Harrell, in the twelve years they've been together, have never missed her twice-yearly public appearances at Dollywood—for a few Christmastime concerts in December, and on opening day in April. My visit coincided with her Christmas concerts, a weekend when Patric and Harrell realized their long-held dream of having a private audience with Dolly. Unlike Michael, Dolly does not dole out these encounters willy-nilly. Patric and Harrell paid dearly for the meeting, which they won at a benefit auction for the Boys and Girls Club of Sevierville, Tennessee (where Dolly went to high school). They thought it would be in poor taste to tell how much they paid, but they did allow that it was more than $2,000, with Harrell excusing the indulgence because "it's for Patric's birthday."

Scheduled to last five minutes, the visit ran to about twenty. Dolly entered the room singing, "Happy birthday, dear Patric / I'm here to serve you," then settled down to look at the porcelain dolls they make in her image, and a photo album of their collection. "She told us, 'All you need is my panties and drawers,'" Harrell said. "But we don't want that. That's too personal." She also chatted on their cell phone with their hairdresser in Texas. Hours later, when Patric noticed that she'd left a lipstick smudge on the phone, "I screamed." (Harrell said, "Little things, little things kinda do weird things to you." For Christmas, they gave the phone with lipstick traces to their hairdresser.)

While they were with Dolly, both men kept their cool. "I didn't want her to think, 'Oh, God, there's two more crazies,'" Patric said. "They protect and don't let her around the fans a lot, so we was tryin' not to act like fans." Harrell went in with just a bit of trepidation—"You never know how famous people really are"—but he came away convinced that "Dolly's just a sweet down-home girl. Like she says, her wigs might be fake, a lot of things might be fake, but her heart is the biggest part of her body, and it is real. It was like we'd known each other all of our lives." Meeting her increased their faith in what they called "her message," which they summarized in tandem:

Harrell said, "Just believe in who you are—"

"—and don't let nobody tell you no different," Patric said.

The meeting also left them with some minor regrets. For Harrell, the only drawback was "we didn't get to stay longer." Patric added, "Sometimes when you meet somebody you've been dreaming about, somebody you've been trying to meet, it kind of takes your breath away. You focus on her so much that you forget what you're actually doing. You lose track of what's happened." Then on to the next wish: "If she would tour the house," he said, "that would be our ultimate dream."

Dolly does make time to meet some fans without requiring charitable donations. One of these is David

Schmidli, thirty-three, of Huntsville, Alabama. For David, who has cerebral palsy, Dolly really is the alpha and omega. His mother Jo-Ann, seventy-two, teaches him to spell with words drawn from Dolly's song titles and lyrics. His sister Lisa, a private detective, suspects that David's fascination with the singer helps fight the progress of his disease. "During family dinners, we could be talking about the war, but he's always back to Dolly, Dolly, Dolly. That's his voice. If it wasn't for her, I don't think David would be the person he is today."

After he had his picture taken with Dolly for the first time, in 1990, David had the snapshot blown up to a life-size cutout. He keeps it in his bedroom, which is decorated with more than one thousand other pictures of the singer. Hers is the first face he sees each morning when he awakens at three-thirty to scour the Web for news of Dolly, then feeds his thoroughbred German shepherd, named Sparkles Dolly Parton, before going to his job as a tester at a computer manufacturing facility. During the holidays, he invites his coworkers home to show them his Christmas tree covered with four hundred homemade ornaments each decorated with Dolly's picture.

David also sharpens his dexterity by making needlepoint tissue-box covers and flyswatter covers bearing Dolly's image (with angel wings). When he presents these items to Dolly each April at the park's opening day, Jo-Ann said, "She's as kind and as good as she can be. She looks down from on high on her float . . . and she says, 'I love you, too, David.'" Lisa said, "She actually deeply, honestly cares. She loves people. She loves David. She honestly does."

David was sitting on a sofa between Jo-Ann and Lisa in the lobby of the Holiday Inn in Pigeon Forge. He wore a jeans jacket covered with butterfly appliqués, over a sweat-shirt decorated with photo iron-ons shaped like Christmas tree ornaments depicting snapshots of "David 'n' Dolly." He has trouble speaking in complete sentences, but he nodded and smiled and occasionally said "Yes" or "Dolly" as his mom and sister spoke. "His greatest dream is to have her come to our house to see his Christmas tree," Jo-Ann said. I asked whether she thought that might happen, and Jo-Ann, alluding to one of Dolly's songs, answered in the knowing, uncynical tone that grown-ups use for talking about Santa Claus: "Think so? In the 'White Limozeen'?"

Tai Uhlman, the director of a documentary about Dolly Parton fans called *For the Love of Dolly*, was shooting footage at Dollywood the weekend I was there. She told me, "You can think whatever you want to about these people, but for them, Dolly is an occasion to express love and compassion and joy and honesty. They can experience these things with a lot of freedom, because they're focused on a kind of imaginary, mythic person. The way they talk about her, she could be Our Lady of Guadalupe."

I was eager to talk with Our Lady about her pilgrims, but her handlers, most of whom are sweet as pie, didn't make it easy.

After much negotiation, we finally set a time, and on my way to the appointment, I came close to freaking out. I wanted to thank Dolly for "I Am Ready," and to tell her what the song had meant to me, but I was afraid to—because I feared it was unprofessional, because there was a chance I'd get choked up, and because sometimes it's kind of terrifying to meet someone you admire a lot. My anxiety was amplified by fresh grief: Mom had died the previous month, and this trip was the first project I had undertaken since. I called a reliably practical writer friend for advice: "Have the interview. At the end, say, 'On a personal note, I just want to tell you . . .' At the very least, it will probably get you another ten minutes with her. You'll make a connection, and you'll also get something from it." I was convinced.

When I showed up for the interview—it had been canceled, and Dolly's majordomo fed me a line of contradictory excuses, starting with "She's too busy" and ending with "She's lost her voice."

I drove back to my motel furious. I ate supper furious. I wanted to commiserate, and so I went to find Tai Uhlman and her documentary crew—a bunch of kind, smart, charming women from Manhattan with whom I'd fallen madly in like that weekend. I told them how the interview had fallen through, and the story of Dolly's song and reading the Bible to my mom and coming out to her, and I was feeling pretty raw, with anger and frustration and neediness. And shame, for how confused I was.

They listened. Then one of them asked a couple of gentle questions: "How do you hope that she might respond if you tell her?" and "Why is it important to you to tell her?"

As I put my muddle of motives into words, I began to realize it didn't matter whether Dolly heard my story. She hears stories like mine every day. If I had told her, she could not possibly have made an adequate response, because my desire to tell my story stemmed from fandom's most essential misconception: that a fan's intimate relationship with an entertainer's work is an intimate relationship with the person who made that work. I started wondering, what must it feel like to hear the millionth story of "how you changed my life," when she knows that she's actually just a tiny sliver of that Great Big Dolly Parton in the Sky?

I didn't need to tell Dolly that story—didn't even want to tell Dolly that story—because the story was mine. The act of reaching out and reading to Mom had been mine, and Dolly did not deserve credit for the understanding I had come to. Dolly sang a song. Then I did something with that song. She made art. I took art and made it into love. I'd been on the verge of using that story as a chit for trade, to get an extra ten minutes of time with Dolly Parton, and I didn't want to use it that way, because it was worth more than that—more than a hit of false intimacy with a star.

And yet, to come to this decision, I needed to pass through every misconception and mistake in this whole chain of events. I had to decide that I could tell her, to get my fear of her out of the way—to imagine myself as occupying a reality that isn't separate and isolated from Dolly's famous life. I had to be told I couldn't speak to her, to get angry about being shut out, and to let all my feelings boil for a while, so that I could realize that, in being cut off from Dolly Parton, I was not really being denied anything I truly needed. My story about how loving that song helped me love my mom better was of infinite worth already. This was my life. And sitting down across from the wig and makeup and plastic surgery and lights and spangles and smiles and boobs and celebrity and telling her about myself would not make my experience more real, wouldn't make my heart learn or heal faster.

I still needed that interview, but I wasn't confused about

why I needed it anymore. That's probably why I finally got it a couple of weeks after my trip to Dollywood. When Dolly called me, I didn't want to tell her about my mom. I wanted to hear how she experiences the relationships that make so many fans believe that she cares for them.

She said, "A lot of times my fans don't come to see me be me. They come to see me be them. They come to hear me say what they want to hear, what they'd like to say themselves, or to say about them what they want to believe is true."

Toward the end of our chat, I said, "People think that they've been healed by you."

She laughed and squealed. "Ha, ha! They do? Well, you know what? I think that, if they do, it's like, people love to respond to love and to energy. That's all about faith anyway, you know. I don't think anybody has the gift of healing unless you have such a gift of love that people can claim enough of that to heal themselves. Certainly I don't claim to be no healer. But I'm a very 'up' person, and I kid and joke, and sometimes I'll say and do crazy stuff almost like a witch doctor that can take people's minds off themselves. And they say, the body will heal itself if it's not dwelling on itself. If you can distract the mind, the body will heal itself . . . I look so weird, it's like they're trying to examine me. 'Oh, God, are they real?' Or, 'How's she walking?' Or, 'Look at them nails.' By the time they get me analyzed, they've forgot about themselves and maybe they have time to do a little healing then . . . Maybe, if there's any healing done, it's because I'm so bizarre and out there that they'll forget themselves for a minute, and while they're gone, their body heals."

She laughed some more, before repeating herself. The

message bears repeating: "It has nothing to do with me. I'm distracting them, while they heal themselves."

Dolly has always believed that she was special. In her memoir, she recalls sitting on her aunt's knee, listening to her sing "Tiptoe tiptoe, little Dolly Parton / Tiptoe tiptoe, ain't she fine . . ." and being "amazed that Aunt Marth knew a song that had my name in it. It never occurred to me you could put anybody's name in the song. And, after all, I was special. Why shouldn't there be a song about a special little girl?" A few years later, Dolly's uniqueness was endorsed in spiritual, even magical, terms: "When I was seven or eight, a woman considered by some in our part of the country to be a saint or a prophet laid her hands on me in church one day. Her eyes were closed. She didn't know whose child she was touching. She said out loud in a clear voice, 'This child is anointed.' I didn't know that word. Disjointed, yes. Anointed, no. I asked Mama what she meant by that. 'You have a mission,' she said. 'God has placed his hand on you, picked you to do some special things in this world, praise him and maybe help people.'"

Locals' feelings about Dolly are complicated. They, too, are fans and view her as an emblem of possibility. "She's as big as a star can get," explained Judge Gary Wade. "If there's a kid who has any talent at all here in town, you can point to Dolly Parton and say, 'She came from here, and that means anything can happen, to anyone who works for it.'" And since she is the county's meal ticket, most negative comments about her are off-the-record. (Sevier County was among the poorest of Tennessee's ninety-five counties when she grew up there; now, thanks largely to Dollywood, it attracts more than two million tourists a

year, and sales tax receipts are among the state's highest.)
Jack Herschend, one of the park's co-owners, proudly
joked, "I think you'd be lynched if you tried to say anything negative about Dolly in this county."

But sometimes heresy slips through. A Dollywood employee who asked not to be identified drew my attention to
a tiny cabin in the amusement park, which is said to be a
replica of the Parton family home: "How could they fit
twelve people in there?" She smirked. "I'd ask her if they
let us talk to her. But they don't let us talk to her."

Most Dollywood employees have little personal contact with the singer. During my visit, for the first time in
four years, she posed for photographs with groups of
employees. On a rainy Friday morning, about a thousand
Dollywood staffers gathered in the park's Showstreet
Palace theater. Fake-stumbling at her entrance, Dolly
got a laugh, then bounded to center stage in five-inch
heels, and the place erupted in cheers and applause.
"What in the world you doin' out in the rain this time
of mornin'?" she teased. "I know! You come out 'cause
you're *crazy*!" She tossed her head and laughed, pulling
strands of her wig from her mouth. "And I got my hair
caught in my lip gloss! Just know that I love you and I
appreciate you."

She stood aside as a Dollywood employee told the
crowd, "You know the drill: no coats, no cameras, no
bags, nothin' to be autographed." For the next hour, Dolly
walked back and forth between bleachers on either side of
the stage, posing with groups of about ten to thirty
employees at a time. Every so often, she took a hair
and makeup break: two attendants hustled onstage and
dolled her up. Watching this, one of Dollywood's pub-

licists bragged, "This is a very well-organized, well-tuned machine."

When the last picture had been snapped, Dolly hollered a down-home "Thank you!" and turned on her heel with queenly efficiency; an assistant covered her shoulders with a woolen cape that billowed as she strode offstage.

For Dolly's fans, the paradoxes of her persona—artificial and authentic, ambitious and altruistic, distant and down-to-earth—hang together. With her, they experience a kind of intimacy that is all the more powerful for being composed largely of illusion.

To be a Dolly Parton fan, a Michael Jackson fan, a fan of almost any star, is to believe in an illusion that provides an exquisite sense of relief. When Dolly was thirteen, she waited in the parking lot of Nashville's Ryman auditorium to meet one of her idols. In her book she writes that it was late at night and she was sleepy. She got sick of waiting and was ready to give up, and then "a man stepped out the stage door and walked over to us . . . and there was no other time. There was only this moment. There was only me and Johnny Cash."

This particular relief is one of fandom's great delights. Encountering our favorite stars, we enter into moments that, as pure *event*, deliver us from tiredness, boredom, and frustration and convince us that there is no other time.

When I asked Dolly if she believed that, she said, "It's a relief, but don't you think it almost becomes like an addiction, too? They get addicted to that feeling. It's almost like how some people fall in love over and over and over just so they can have that one feeling. They'll fall out of love so they can go get somebody new so they can have that feeling again.

With a real fan, they have those moments that make them feel that. Maybe a different moment at each concert. Some of these fans have seen my concerts over and over, even know almost every word I'm gonna say, every note I'm gonna play, every joke I'm gonna tell, but there'll be something new I do in every show, or some new move I'll make, and I'll have people say that 'oh. I never heard you tell that before.' 'Oh, I never saw that,' 'Oh . . .' It's almost like they wait for those little magic moments. I feel it from the crowd, too, which, that gives *me* a rush."

For some, like those of Michael's lost girls who seek to salve their loneliness in fleeting moments of contact with a person they will never really know, fandom may well be a malignant addiction. Many other fans, like Thomasina and David and Patric and Harrell, find ways to use their feelings about celebrities to help solve problems—in ways that may not be ideal, but are effective. What happens when these fans get close to fame may be as transitory and deceptive as a drug trip, but it is still a human encounter. And anticipating these encounters and remembering them are among fans' most powerful weapons for doing battle with the things in life that would keep us down.

As sites of pilgrimage, Dollywood and Neverland give material expression to the idea that fandom is a creative space: a playground of the mind and spirit, a construction site of the self. At the same time, these pilgrimages are costly endeavors, for everyone involved. On both sides of relationships between stars and fans, parts of people always get used up.

Q. Last question: In your autobiography, you wrote, "Love is what it has always been about. The reason for wanting to be a star was to be able to create more love and share it with more people." Do you have a general sense, a gut feeling, as to whether the emotions that bind you and your fans really are love, or whether they're something else—whether they're more healthy or more unhealthy?

A. Well, that's a very good and involved question. I think that there's some of all that. I've often wondered if it's healthy for some of these people to depend on me that much to where people live through you and don't live their own lives. I often worry about that. It's like when people say "I'm in love" when they're really in lust. They call so many things love. But I truly believe that those true fans find a place in themselves, that if there is love in them, they truly take that on. Now some of it gets distorted, granted, it does. And for myself, I know that some people, some fans, are easier to tolerate than others. I mean, it's a big responsibility. It's almost like bein' a teacher. You have all kinds of students. Some of 'em get on your nerves more than others. Some of 'em, you really try to say, "You don't need to be worshiping me, because I don't believe in idol gods, false gods." I'm always very careful not to lead people astray that don't really have that much strength of their own or know their own true identity, to where they just live through you. Certainly I'm just speaking for myself and my fans at the moment, but I think that for my fans that have been around a long time, they see enough stuff in me that I truly want to believe that a part of them really comes to love me. And I think that definitely there's other stuff that's so cluttered up that I couldn't even begin to try to analyze all of that nor to sort it out because I'm not a therapist. But I do think about it. I do analyze a lot of stuff. I spend a lot of time thinking about stuff like that in the wee hours. About how things happen, how people are the way that they are, and, like you say, is it healthy? Is it not healthy? But I think it's healthier for those people to have something to look forward to than to not. Because if they've got a show to look forward to going to or a record to look forward to coming out, it might keep them from doing something bad to themselves or to somebody else. Like suicide. Or to keep 'em off the streets. Or give 'em something more to do than just dwelling on themselves so much. I don't know. I just know I love the fans. I appreciate 'em. I love what I do. So I guess we'll all be at it for a long time to come.

3

Not Just at the Scene, Part of It

VERTICAL STRINGS OF GREEN apples—seven thousand in all—formed the backdrop to the bar at Larry King's seventieth birthday party on a cool November night in Beverly Hills, the same week that Michael Jackson was arrested on charges of child molestation. The party's "ambience designer," Edgardo Zamora, said that Larry's wife, Shawn, had helped to inspire the decoration because she loves Granny Smith apples. But the strings of green triggered a different association for a publicist friend of mine, who said, "Doesn't it look just like the numbers in *The Matrix*?"

At six, the first wave of guests arrived at the Museum of Television & Radio to watch the broadcast of *Larry King Live*. The birthday boy appeared to be genuinely shocked when his interview with Regis Philbin (Q: "What do you make of this Jackson story?" A: "I kind of feel sorry for everyone involved") was hijacked by Dr. Phil and transformed into a tribute, à la *This Is Your Life*, with satellite feeds and phone calls from the likes of Nancy Reagan, Ross Perot (with the Dallas Cowboy Cheerleaders), and Celine Dion (singing "Happy Birthday," backed up by her four-thousand-member audience in Las Vegas). Clustered in front of one television set were Larry King's personal assistant, his personal assistant's mother, his sister-in-law, and his mother-in-law. Behind them stood two balding men from Sweden.

Pekka Johansson, who like most men at the party was wearing black socks, but unlike any other man at the party was wearing shorts, and Ingmar Ohman, who was the only man there wearing sandals, said they were freelance writers, visiting town for two weeks to "see how Hollywood works." They are both regular contributors to a Swedish magazine called *Music and Audio Technology*, and they said they had not yet decided whether they would try to write a story about Larry King's birthday party. I delicately asked what, then, they were doing here.

"He's like number one in news, right?" Pekka said.

"Yeah, isn't he?" Ingmar said.

"We more or less just walked by here earlier this afternoon," Pekka said. "We presented ourselves at the front desk, and they said, 'Why don't you come by here later?' "

The second wave of guests began arriving just after six-thirty. The first guests to trigger a flash of lights from the TV crews in the arrival area were former California governor Gray Davis (who'd just lost the recall election to Arnold Schwarzenegger) and his wife, Sharon. They chatted for a while with Kaye Coleman, the waitress who serves Larry King's breakfast most mornings at Nate & Al's, a diner in Beverly Hills. Shortly thereafter, *Laugh-In* producer George Schlatter wrapped Priscilla Presley in a bear hug and said, "We *are* gonna have that lunch! We *are* gonna have that lunch!"

I asked Priscilla how long she had known Larry King, and she said, "Larry's been around for a while. We've all grown up with him." Her hair, auburn with yellow streaks, framed her face in such a way that she seemed to be peeking out from among the wild grasses of the veld. "I think he's a wonderful interviewer. I think he's very personable. I think he's very interested in what one has to say. He does it without being so invasive."

Barbara Eden, in a stop-sign-red pantsuit with twinkly stars sewn on, said that she had come to Larry King's party "because I love him."

Why do you love him?

"Because he's a wonderful man."

What's wonderful about him?

"I think he's a very good person."

Don Rickles, looking dapper with a crimson pocket square in his navy blazer, was seated on an aqua leather chair. He said, "Larry King is a very down-to-earth guy. He has a wonderful role with people of importance, and yet he can still hang with the guys. He's one of us, as I am one of him. So be it."

The guest of honor, who had been led to believe that he would be having a quiet dinner with his wife at the Peninsula Hotel, arrived at the surprise party and made his way upstairs, where Burt Bacharach was hanging out on the landing. A camera crew from *60 Minutes II* rolled tape as Pekka and Ingmar approached Larry to say, with swooping inflection, "Congratulations from Sweden. You are our media hero."

Just before he went onto the dance floor that had been erected under a tent outside, Larry talked to me about his evening so far: "Tonight was a total whack-out. I was totally prepared to go for the hour with Regis. But then, Oprah and Cher and Madonna and Sharon Stone. I couldn't believe it." He continued a litany of names that scrambled the well-known and the unfamiliar, making no distinction between those who appeared via satellite and those who showed up in person: "Kaye from Nate and Al's, my first producer, my best friend Herbie from Washington. Tim Robbins—"

"Tony Robbins," his publicist corrected.

"—Tony Robbins—Ted Olson the solicitor general, Colin Powell."

Then, after the crowd sang "Happy Birthday" and before he cut the cake, Larry King grabbed a microphone and looked out at all of the most important people in his life and teased them, because he had gotten fooled— "There are so many liars in this room!"—and when I looked around, every face I saw was laughing.

Dishonesty, in one form or another, is an occupational requirement for entertainment journalists—the men and women who straddle the Wall of Fame, the ones who purport to show the rest of the world what it's really like in the dreamland of Hollywood. To gain access to that world, journalists habitually misrepresent themselves, sometimes by playing the role of starstruck fan, and sometimes by pretending to be blasé. Once granted access, it's expected that journalists will also bend the truth to help their subjects look good or at least be sure to suppress any potentially damaging information. Larry King, like his colleagues and Swedish admirers manqué, is above all else a flatterer.

There's no way to cure the mendacity of entertainment journalism, because the dishonesty of this profession has a chicken/egg relationship to the fantasies of fandom. Most entertainment journalists are people who grew up in thrall to Hollywood. When we start poking around backstage, it quickly becomes clear that life in starworld isn't what it's cracked up to be, and yet the appetites of our readers and viewers—and sometimes, our own abiding desire to see celebrities as somehow greater than standard-issue human beings—make it practically impossible to give a fully truthful account of what we learn in this world, even if we want to.

Imagine, for instance, that a magazine sends you to interview an actor whom most of America would view as a hero. The guy turns out to be nice, polite, and dumb as a doorknob. When you ask him where he grew up, he says, with much brow-furrowing, words to the effect of *It was a place called . . . It was called—no . . . Wow. I haven't been asked this question in—um. I can't remember where it is. There's Austin, Texas, but it wasn't there, it was . . . I don't mind telling you, I just seriously can't—oh! Fort Worth! That's what it is!*

Imagine turning this in to your editor, thinking that it's fairly noteworthy that our hero can't remember the name of the town where he spent his formative years, and your editor sending back the story with the quote reduced to two words: *Fort Worth.* Your assignment was to write the piece in Q&A format, which common sense would suggest is basically just a cleaned-up transcript of a conversation more or less as it actually happened. But the Q&A your editor sends back to you has remixed the chronology: the end is at the beginning, the beginning at the end. Grammar and word choice have been sharpened and fragments fused together, to form a flow of meaning as smooth and casually intimidating as the actor's on-screen image. The essence of your conversation hasn't changed, but anything humanly ragged or rambling or jumpy or strange has been filed down, sharpened, focused.

You could make a fuss over the changes, but that would probably mean the magazine wouldn't give you more work; and your rent's about to come due. And after all, is anything precious being lost if we just fly past the hero's ignorance of the name of the town where he learned to fire spitballs or fold paper airplanes? Isn't it possible that we're really doing readers some kind of service when we let them go on believing this guy's actually smarter than a door-knob? After all, the Q&A tells something close enough to the truth to be acceptable, and your conversation hasn't been so much revised as redesigned, using nothing but the lightest, whitest kinds of lies as tools.

You have been conscripted by the forces that make and keep this man a star. You made him look good. In a small way now, you've become part of the show. And even if the process makes you kind of queasy—because you're working for a respected editor at a trusted publication—still, seeing how it works is kind of fun. It makes you feel special, even if you know that feeling is petty, to have this funny story all to yourself, to tell your friends as a way of showing them how inside you are. Plus, by telling them, you get to reassure yourself that, even if you've been conscripted, there's a part of you that hasn't been co-opted. You're retelling the story to show that you're more honest and truthful, and above all more innocent, than the jaded editors you work for.

But casting yourself as the innocent gets a little harder when this kind of thing happens the next time. Or the next. Or the time after that. Every time it happens, you under-stand a little more clearly that a whole industry of people have done this so many times they've lost count, have developed systems and rules and standards of misrepresentation. Holidays in this world—like the Sundance Film Festival (of which more later) or the TV Critics Association Press Tour (a biannual, two-week extravaganza where the casts of network series mingle with print journalists on the TV beat)—make their celebrants feel so seemingly chummy with stars that the Wall of Fame can seem as insubstantial as the northern lights.

Paradoxically, it's these experiences, which are granted mostly to the jaded, that have the most power to restore one's starstruck innocence—even though that innocence is almost always undermined at the same time. At my first TV critics' press tour I met a writer for *TV Guide*, whose world-weary aspect cracked when he confessed, "I'm here to meet the people I love." When I asked him to tell me about the biggest thrill he had ever had at this event, he said, "The first night of my first press tour, we were having dinner with the cast of *90210*. *Melrose Place* was at the next table. I was in heaven. My editor said, 'Should I call the paramedics now?' I was saying, 'I can't eat. I'm talking to Jennie Garth.' And I really literally didn't eat anything. Then at the end of the night I went up to get some dessert and there was literally one cookie left. And Luke Perry came up at the same time and we were both standing there, and he was like, 'Do you mind?' I said no, and we stood there talking. And he ate the whole cookie."

Imagine long hours listening to such stories, learning axioms of the entertainment journalist's life, like *Luke Perry will always get the whole cookie* and *You will always watch him eat it*. And imagine that, around the time you think you're learning the rules of the game, you meet a well-known TV entertainment reporter who doesn't know you from Adam, who's complaining about "the bullshit," and you nod, thinking you know what he's talking about, and then he says that several years ago his producers acquired a compromising videotape of Michael Jackson, and "I just didn't know what to do. They said they couldn't give it to the authorities because they didn't want Sony Records to turn against them. That was a hard one for me."

You ask, so what did you do?

He says, "I went along with it. I had no choice. I have to keep my job. I have to feed my kids."

When you don't say anything right away, he asks, "What? What do you think? Do I sound like a sellout?"

The first fan magazine, *Photoplay*, included a gossip column with the candid headline FACTS AND NEAR-FACTS ABOUT THE GREAT AND NEAR-GREAT OF FILMLAND. Since then, entertainment journalists have rarely been so open regarding their complex relationship to the truth. Louella Parsons and Hedda Hopper, the gossip columnists who made a show of running Hollywood in its golden age, were basically establishment lackeys, mostly repeating stories spoon-fed to them by studio publicists. (In fact, Louella probably owed her career to a cover-up. She was among those on William Randolph Hearst's yacht for the 1924 cruise on which producer and director Thomas Ince was murdered, possibly by Charlie Chaplin. Soon after the incident, she claimed to have been in New York at the time and was subsequently awarded a lifetime contract with Hearst's newspapers.) When Columbia Pictures chief Harry Cohn wanted *Confidential*, the 1950s scandal magazine, to keep a lid on the truth of Rock Hudson's sex life, he offered them gossip about one of his lesser stars,

Rory Calhoun. *Confidential* obliged, and the magazine's double-dealing relationship with Columbia endured.

For many Hollywood journalists, duplicity is merely expedient. It can also express a desire to be liked by the people we envy. Many of us are, at heart, the kind of fans who once wished we could be stars. One prime example was Rona Barrett, who in 1966 became the first Hollywood gossip columnist to have her own segment on a local TV newscast and later moved on to *Good Morning America*, *The Tomorrow Show*, and *Entertainment Tonight*. (She now runs a lavender farm near Santa Barbara.) The daughter of a grocery store owner and a housewife in Queens, Rona Burstein was an overweight child who wore a leg brace because she suffered from a form of muscular dystrophy. In her autobiography, *Miss Rona*, she remembered dreaming of fame as revenge when she was teased by the kids at her school: "Someday, so help me, I'll be so important . . . so famous . . . none of you will ever be able to touch me again!"

In the meantime, thirteen-year-old Rona started making herself into a Somebody. She took the subway into Manhattan, found her way to Eddie Fisher's manager's office, introduced herself as Rona "Barrett," and persuaded the manager to let her start the first Eddie Fisher Fan Club. Soon she moved on to the Steve Lawrence Fan Club, then dropped out of college when she was eighteen to work for a fanzine. Within a few years, she had lost the leg brace, moved to Los Angeles, and remade herself in the image of a star. Following the path of Rita Hayworth's transformation, she raised her hairline with electrolysis, then sought out Kim Novak's masseuse to help her lose weight.

Her first gossip column, for a magazine called *Motion Picture*, taught Rona the dangers of indiscretion, after an item about her friend Frankie Avalon cost her their friendship. Rona soon sharpened her powers of suppression, as did most Hollywood journalists who knew what was good for them. *Dish* (2000), the history of gossip by MSNBC columnist Jeannette Walls, amply documents the culture of misrepresentation created in the murky territory between journalism and fandom. In the 1970s, for instance, *People* had a policy of being "very, very careful about what we let people say," according to editor Dick Stolley. Prudently, they discovered and buried truckloads of dirt on the magazine's best-selling cover subject of that decade, Cher. (She and Sonny got matching nose jobs, etc.)

When Elvis Presley died in 1977, the news media were amazed by the public demand for details of his demise. In the frenzy of competition, journalists grew scrappier and more confrontational with celebrities—a transition that was marked, for some, by considerable anguish. A fan's adoration collided with a journalist's bloodlust when *Rolling Stone* founder Jann Wenner was informed of the King's death. The magazine's music editor Peter Herbst recalled delivering the news to Wenner, who scrunched up his face and began to cry: "These tears were rolling down his face, and he was trying to say something, but I couldn't understand." Finally, Wenner managed to make himself understood over the sound of his own sobbing: "It's . . . It's a cover [story]."

Every journalist covering the story wanted to view Elvis Presley's body at Graceland, but reporters were barred from the estate. So the *New York Post* sent one of its interns—Caroline Kennedy—to Memphis. The singer's family, believing that the late president's daughter had come to show her respects, immediately welcomed her. (Her story was killed by the *Post*, apparently because it lacked color and insight, but *Rolling Stone* snapped it up.) Caroline Kennedy's exclusive demonstrated another rule of entertainment journalism: if you want access to the inner sanctum of celebrity, the most valuable credential is celebrity itself—because every gatekeeper in the labyrinth of fame is a fan.

A few journalists, such as Barbara Walters (whose salary hit the $1 million mark in 1976), had already begun creating their own form of celebrity; and when *20/20* debuted on ABC in 1978, its reporters included names like Geraldo Rivera and, later, Ron Reagan Jr. Celebrity-staffed, celebrity-friendly tabloid television became a hit for the networks.

In 1981, television cooked up another new genre of entertainment journalism—the syndicated daily Hollywood news show—in the form of *Entertainment Tonight*. The show's innovation was simple: by reporting box office grosses and development deals—the kinds of facts that, before the Internet, were all but unknown to people in middle America—*Entertainment Tonight* made daily news from Hollywood more accessible to more fans than ever before.

Today, *ET* vies for attention with a crowd of imitators, such as *Access Hollywood*, *E! News Daily*, and *Extra!* It even has its own spin-off, *The Insider*. Yet *ET* is still the country's top-rated syndicated newsmagazine, with national ratings almost half again as strong as its closest competitor and an audience that extends far beyond the entertainment news niche. In the most coveted viewer demographic, eighteen-to-forty-nine-year-olds, *Entertainment Tonight* beats the ABC, NBC, and CBS newscasts hands down.

Within a year of its launch, *ET* found an anchor who is still, for much of America, an icon of the ultimate Hollywood insider—a fan from South Dakota whose own dreams of acting stardom, though frustrated, would lead to a resplendent, twenty-two-and-counting-year reign as the world's friendliest entertainment journalist. Mary Hart's reassuring, affable, and ever-enthusiastic demeanor is the foundation of her show's success. Jim Van Messel, a former executive producer of *ET* and the creator of *Access Hollywood*, told me, "As far as the folks at home know, Mary Hart has never had a bad day. Her self-imposed mandate is to make people feel a little better about the day through *Entertainment Tonight*. She is the Mr. Rogers of syndicated television."

When I was growing up, that's what she was to me. Every day I would come home from school and *ET* would keep me company while I sat at my desk in the living room, writing letters to famous people. One broadcast that I'll never forget was on my fifteenth birthday, October 2, 1985, when Mary Hart told me that Rock Hudson had died of AIDS. She wore a magenta dress the same color as the background of the show's credits, and she read the news with her chin angled lower than usual, in a serious voice (which was basically the normal Mary, minus the smile, with the bass jacked up a couple notches).

Rock Hudson had been the only strong, masculine man whom I'd ever heard was gay—and since I spent a huge number of hours suppressing the question of whether I was that way, too, I had had mixed feelings about his announcement, a while earlier, that he had AIDS. On the one hand, it had been a relief, because (even though he died in the closet) you couldn't look away from the fact that this strong man was probably a homo. On the other hand, the news had been torture, for exactly the same reason: if a real man like Rock Hudson was gay, there would be one thing less to stop me from imagining being that way myself—a frightening prospect in a town where fully one quarter of the boys at school dressed for the football team. So I had the same mix of emotions about his death, although I remember my own feelings that day with less precision than I remember Mary Hart's comforting presence.

Recently, I looked at that episode again. Mary's empathic manner was exactly as I'd remembered, but my memory had edited out another important segment of the program. Halfway through the show, Rona Barrett came on-screen to deliver a remembrance of Rock. She recollected having cried her eyes out while watching him on-screen in *Magnificent Obsession*, not imagining that she would one day interview and become friends with him. "He always loved his privacy and clung to it like a tiger," she said. "In the late sixties there was a widely printed rumor about a relationship between Hudson and another popular actor." In response, "Rock simply outclassed everyone spreading this filth and ignored the attack." Moments later, Rona alluded to a "recent explosion of press speculation about Rock's private life after the disclosure that he had AIDS" and with admiration, explained, "Again, he chose to rise above the situation and concentrate on what was important: his fight against this deadly disease."

When he died, Rock Hudson's sexuality was still off-the-record, so his "friend" Rona can't be faulted for keeping his secret. Still, there's something breathtakingly, nimbly corrupt about her distorted remembrance of him. She could have just let his secret alone, but instead she chose deliberately to mislead her audience. She looked straight into the camera and said the truth was "filth."

Then Mary Hart said, "Thank you, Rona" in her serious voice, as if Rona had just said something genuine and profound, and the program went on.

What did Rock Hudson's lies, and Rona Barrett's defense of those lies, and Mary Hart's tacit assent to them, do to me as a fifteen-year-old kid? In the strictest view, these falsehoods matter because so many believe that stars are models of what it is to be a person, archetypes of the kinds of lives we can live. Journalism that hides the truth by avoiding sensitive topics—even the trivial: letting supermodels get away with claims they live on pizza and ice cream, never asking Ricky Martin who he's dating—helps to build false idols whose lives present impossible standards for the rest of us, and to create an incoherent picture of success and happiness that breeds frustration for celebrities and fans alike.

Years ago, when an interviewer supposedly said, "Everybody would like to be Cary Grant," Cary Grant is supposed to have replied, "So would I." The exchange has become a cliché because it's an amusing, poignant measure of the distance between an actor's public image and his private self. It also sticks in the memory for a more complicated reason: it pretends to be surprising even though it just confirms something already known. Cary Grant suggests that he's just like the rest of us, with a clipped, urbane rejoinder that's classic Cary Grant. We take comfort in his comment, even as it puts us in our place. There's real pleasure in this mixture of reassurance and humiliation, similar to the pleasure that Cary Grant's on-screen persona offered the leading ladies that he loved but often didn't treat so well.

The cocktail of reassurance and humiliation is one of pop culture's specialty drinks. Fans love it. I got hooked early on, and by the time I was fifteen, I found the pleasure of Mary Hart's reassurance so great that I barely flinched when Rona smeared the truth. When something that makes you feel bad is also the thing that best helps you feel better, it's hard even to imagine the prospect of giving it up.

For a while I was asking everyone I talked to if they had any good stories about Mary Hart, and I found that no one who had met her—even the people who didn't respect her work, or those who wondered out loud if she is actually animatronic—had a single nasty word to say about her. When I asked Jeannette Walls if any off-color or salacious rumors about Mary have ever circulated in Hollywood, she wailed, "Nooo!" The guy who works at my local video store said he once opened a door at a shopping mall and accidentally slammed it into Mary. "It must have hurt, but she just started laughing and picking up all the bags full of stuff that she dropped and said, 'Oh my! I'm so sorry! Excuse me!' "

Thanks in part to such reflexive, sunny poise, Mary's relationships with her subjects are as cozy as those of any journalist in Hollywood's history. Is it possible that she doesn't have a dark side? Producer Jim Van Messel said, "She's pretty simple. There's not a lot of complexity to her.

She's just plain Mary." He paused, then added, "Mary has been in Hollywood for twenty years, so she has learned how to swim with the sharks. If plain Mary didn't know how to swim with the sharks, there'd be no plain Mary." That tension, which sustains her success, may be rooted in a deeper tension that has fueled it. From early childhood, she's moved back and forth between wanting to be a star, and wanting to be a regular person who lives among the stars. (After the telecast of Mary Martin's *Peter Pan*, young Mary Hart directed plays with her brothers, keeping two roles for herself—Peter, for whom life is all fun and fairy dust, and Wendy, who becomes a responsible grownup.) She's a starry-eyed pragmatist, simple yet shrewd. I wanted to meet her, to ask how being a fan has influenced her career. I wanted to see firsthand how much of her innocent image is an act, and whether she, like other top Hollywood journalists, has gotten rich by being economical with the truth.

So I persuaded an editor to let me write a profile of her and then started calling her publicists, twins David and Sandy Brokaw, bugging them for months until we nailed down a day that I could spend with Mary. When I found out that *Entertainment Tonight* is taped at Paramount Studios, I realized that I was bound for the same place that Ray Bradbury had described to me when I began this odyssey. To meet her, I'd have to go past the same wall that he did. I'd have to jump over the wall of Paramount and land inside and come back with a story.

Before the sun came up one morning in May 2002, Sandy Brokaw drove me to Paramount. He insisted on driving because I was new to Los Angeles, and he was worried about my getting lost and being late. Sandy was the first publicist I'd ever met, and he was old school: a short guy in a checkered sport coat, with gray hair and small features. My first thought on getting into his car, a big old American sedan, was that he looked like a rabbit.

The car slowed to a stop at the studio's arched, wrought-iron gate. "Where should we park?" Sandy asked the guard. "Sky?"

"Down by the sky," said the guard. I was completely disoriented, but my confusion went away as we drove toward a gigantic billboard backdrop painted pale blue with clouds and found an empty space to put the car.

We walked back up toward the entrance, past the gift shop and the commissary, with its lit glass showcases of Oscars out front, and then down a row of soundstages to the Mae West building, where Reginald Foster ("six foot five, two hundred and forty pounds. Don't sell me short"), Mary's security guard, was waiting at the door. I met her assistant Laurie Iverson, whose computer desktop wallpaper was a detail from the creation scene of Michelangelo's Sistine Chapel, and who was a dead ringer for Laura Dern ("When she has a movie out, my life is living hell").

Then I turned a corner into a pale pink office where I saw Mary, in a black mock-turtleneck sweater and trousers, behind a wooden desk painted white, pink, and gold, with a satin-lined, leopard-print jacket slung over the back of her chair. There was no computer in sight. "It's five o'clock in the morning!" she said, gesturing to Reggie and Laurie. "I forced them to get up. And everybody's happy!"

Her natural effervescence enhanced by a twenty-ounce, nonfat latte, Mary was surrounded by vases of silk flowers and pictures of herself interviewing celebrities of every stripe: Tom Brokaw, Cher, Dan Quayle, Lee Iacocca, Billy Graham, Arnold Schwarzenegger. It was sweeps week, and she was busy promoting that evening's installment of *Entertainment Tonight* in nine back-to-back radio interviews with morning deejays from stations across the country.

Between interviews, she confessed to a bit of performance anxiety. After one deejay asked about the pop-punk group Blink-182, she said, "I'm always afraid I'll say Blink-152, or Fahrenheit 415." She dished Fran Drescher, who was appearing on *ET* that day to promote a book about her battle with ovarian cancer. "She got over herself," Mary said. "She's lighter. Humbled."

The show's executive producer, Linda Bell Blue, large and formidable in a loud purple blouse, with pale blue eyes set far apart on her wide face, came tearing into the office: "Good ratings last night, kiddo!" She turned to me and said, "This is the entertainment show of record. For millions of women. People."

I'd love to hear more about that, I said. You think of this as a show for women?

"It is innately interesting to women," she said robustly. "Outfits. Marriages. Births"—and she was gone.

During the phone interviews, Mary peered across the room through little oval spectacles, tracking the CNBC stock ticker at the bottom of a television screen housed in a wooden cabinet painted with roses, which stood next to a red velvet sofa draped with a blanket woven with the pattern of the American flag. She moved only the lower part of her face as she talked with the deejays: her eyes and forehead stayed fixed and expressionless, and enough little natural wrinkles were on her face that Botox can probably be ruled out as the reason. (The affect broke just once, when a deejay described Fran Drescher as "the Lucille Ball of our time," and Mary's eyes narrowed to small slits.)

The disc jockeys told her, "You're a babe." They sang the *ET* theme song, repeatedly. They asked, "How's life in la-la land?" and, since *Spider-Man* had opened the previous weekend, "Where does Tobey Maguire live?" and "How's Kirsten Dunst?" Mary told one that she'd stood in line with her son for forty minutes to get her ticket to *Spider-Man*, "just like everybody else." Hadn't she heard that people were camping out all night to get tickets? What did she think of that? "Those are homeless people," she joked, pretending to scold. Another deejay said, "You should stop calling it *Entertainment Tonight*. It's *Entertainment Forever!*"

The deejays treated her with a strange mixture of deference and familiarity, as if unsure whether to address Mary Hart as a fellow worker in the broadcast industry or as a celebrity in her own right. Their confusion made perfect sense to me. She's one of the most powerful journalists in Hollywood's industry of personhood. But what kind of a person is she?

According to Leo Braudy, most of television's celebrity journalists fall into one of two categories. He thinks Mary currently fills a role perfected by Johnny Carson, "the normal person who is our interlocutor with the world of fame." Figures such as Barbara Walters, he said, are "more given to hype, pushing towards being as much a celebrity as the celebrities themselves." The categories tend to blur, however. Of Mary, he said, "It is almost inevitable that the interlocutor become a celebrity, too. But she has to preserve the connection with her audience. She has to be a bridge."

Like a lot of normal people, Mary Hart had an unusual upbringing. Born Mary Johanna Harum in 1951, the daughter of a Lutheran farm-implement dealer and a housewife, her family moved eleven times in South Dakota before she was eight years old. When she was nine, they moved again—to Copenhagen, where she learned Danish; and a few years later to Sweden, where she learned that country's language, too, before she was sent back home to boarding school in South Dakota when she was fifteen. Perhaps because of all the wandering, Mary became extremely assertive, self-possessed, and competitive. Her father, Rob Harum, remembers that she would play Monopoly against herself and then get angry when one of her hands had to lose.

One constant in Mary's life was her love for stars. She was an avid reader of *Confidential*, especially keen on its blow-by-blow accounts of the soap opera loves of Richard Burton, Elizabeth Taylor, Eddie Fisher, and Debbie Reynolds. Still, dreaming about stars wasn't enough for her. She also wanted to meet them. When she was fourteen, she said, she persuaded her father to take her to a Beatles concert in Sweden, where she talked her way backstage and found herself face-to-face with Paul McCartney. Having gotten to where she wanted to be, she didn't know what to do: she felt like fainting, or running. Instead, to her surprise, "all I could think was, 'Okay, ask questions.' He had just come back from the first American tour, so I asked him what he thought of the

United States. How was it? How were the fans different? Would you like to go back? And I probably was stuttering." I asked whether she remembered Paul McCartney's answers, and she said, "I don't remember. I remember him being very nice. I remember him saying that they had a great time and that they loved America. So I do—I do remember that."

While a student at Augustana College in Sioux Falls, South Dakota, she was a runner-up in the 1971 Miss America pageant. After graduating the next year, she worked as a high school English teacher in Sioux Falls and simultaneously produced, directed, and hosted her own local TV show, which led to increasingly prominent jobs on TV news and talk shows in Iowa and Oklahoma. In tapes of these shows, she speaks with an endearing Dakota twang that faded as she spent more time on camera, but is still discernible from time to time in casual conversation.

In 1979, she decided to leave journalism behind. She drove to Los Angeles with $10,000 in the bank and big dreams of acting stardom. "I didn't want to report on the business," she explained. "I wanted to have my own show to be reported on." Living in Westwood, she would jog through the swank neighborhoods of Holmby Hills and Beverly Hills like an explorer claiming her territory, repeating a mantra of self-improvement. "I consciously said to myself every day, 'Someday I will be successful enough to live in this neighborhood,' visualizing myself in that community of success," she said. (She does live in one of those neighborhoods now, with her husband, Burt Sugarman, the producer of the films *Children of a Lesser God* and *Crimes of the Heart*. They have one son, A.J., who appeared on *Entertainment Tonight* the day after he was brought home from the hospital in 1992.)

She landed a few national commercials and played a minor role in several episodes of the soap opera *Days of Our Lives*, but after two years of auditions, Mary's vision wasn't panning out. Nearly out of money, she became hostess of *PM Magazine*, an L.A. news program, which led to a job late in 1981 as co-host of Regis Philbin's first national talk show. When that show was canceled four months later, *Entertainment Tonight* interviewed her about what it felt like to be canned. The day after the interview, *ET* offered her a job as a correspondent; thirteen weeks later, she was named the show's permanent co-host.

She focused on building *ET* as a business from the start and took a leading role in extending its syndication reach while cable television was still in its infancy. (*Entertainment Tonight* and MTV debuted the same year.) Each week after Friday's taping, Mary would fly to Detroit, Birmingham, Houston, and every other midsize TV market in the country to pitch the show to local station managers.

It was a tough sell because *ET* was not only pioneering a new kind of content; it proposed a new form of delivery as well. *Entertainment Tonight* was the first syndicated program to send its shows to stations via satellite every day. Paramount sweetened the deal by offering a free satellite dish to every station that bought the show, but *Entertainment Tonight* was still considered a risky venture.

Gradually, *ET* gained credibility. The networks' evening news shows picked up its footage of the trial following the fatal accident on the set of the *Twilight Zone* movie in 1982. Even Walter Cronkite lauded *Entertainment Tonight* as "one of the best news shows on the air today" and cited its rigorous reporting of "the five w's" in a 1986 interview with the *Washington Post*. (He later told me that he'd stopped watching *ET* when it started running opposite *The Lehrer Report* in New York. He added, "I thought Mary Hart was pretty delightful. Her appearance, primarily. She's very attractive. She also enunciated well, which was in contrast to some of the on-air personalities of the time.")

Ratings climbed, and Mary became famous for reporting on the famous. Her legs were insured for $1 million. In 1991, the *New England Journal of Medicine* reported that her voice triggered seizures in an epileptic woman in New York, a case that later inspired a classic *Seinfeld* episode. She weathered five co-hosts (Ron Hendren, who was replaced in 1984 by Robb Weller, who was replaced in 1986 by John Tesh, who was replaced in 1996 by Bob Goen, who was replaced by Mark Steines, the present co-anchor, in 2004). Even as *Entertainment Tonight* made Mary Hart a household name, however, her old dream of acting stardom didn't go away. She made exercise videos, worked as a motivational speaker, walked the tightrope on *Circus of the Stars*, and shot guest appearances on nighttime series (including the pilot of *Moonlighting*), always playing herself. In 1988, critics creamed her for a Las Vegas lounge act, and stung by the experience, she made *ET* her sole professional focus again, with renewed intensity.

The story of Mary Hart's career is one of constant striving. She tried so hard to be an actress, made almost superhuman efforts to become a kind of celebrity that might have commanded more respect than the world is willing to give an entertainment journalist. Then she finally stopped trying to cross the bridge from the black-and-white world to the color world and realized that she *was* the bridge. "What I learned was that ultimately I am in the best place that I can be in," she said. "I knew this job was good and I knew it was fun, being thrust into the middle of all these situations that I dreamed about. But just in a different way than I'd dreamed about."

In interviews, I tend to speak slowly, feeling my way along the rope of a sentence for what the next word might be. After someone answers a question, I sometimes have to pause to think, and my pauses can last as long as it takes you to tie both of your shoes. In the past, when I'd interviewed people like politicians, authors, or schoolteachers, these pauses had never seemed too awkward, so I was surprised when, with Mary, each silence would trigger a fine mist of sweat on the back of my neck. Talking to her was like this: When I asked a question, she began speaking immediately (even when it took her a while to arrive at her answer) and finished without ever breaking eye contact; then if I needed a second to think, I would form a close-lipped encouraging half-smile and make some kind of *hm* noise, and she would keep staring at me, her eyebrows lowered one meaningful millimeter or so (was the look judgmental, or attentive? I was never quite sure), until my mouth began pronouncing some response. She answered every question without ever taking a break for reflective silence, and she seemed bewildered, even a touch put off, when I had to do so.

To be fair: Mary was the first famous person I interviewed in Hollywood, and the conversational style of a TV journalist has to be quick-fire, not contemplative. These two things probably explain my cervical perspiration, perception of conversational rhythm, and meticulously and arguably overly sensitive interpretation of same. Another observation about her conversational style, however, can't be discredited by my being starstruck.

In her work for *Entertainment Tonight*, she has to talk knowledgeably and knowingly with some of the most famous and powerful people in Hollywood, in an idiom that every fan, everywhere, can understand. She succeeds at this not only, or even primarily, because she is so nice, but because she is sharp about business. Whenever Mary Hart talks about or to a star, even if the immediate topic is battling with ovarian cancer or the birth of a child, she is also selling that star to the public. If you listen closely to her, you begin to realize that she seems never to lose sight of this. Whenever Mary Hart talks about a star, or whenever she is talking about the experience of entertainment, she is talking about economic value.

The first time I noticed this we were talking, appropriately enough, about the experience of being starstruck. She said that the first celebrity sighting that took her breath away happened during her first year in L.A., when she went to Dominic's restaurant in Beverly Hills and saw a silver-haired man standing by the jukebox, and it was Cary Grant.

I responded with the broad question "Are you a fan?" Her answer was animated, rapid, and automatic:

Oh, yes. You heard me talk about Tobey Maguire all morning. I thought he was wonderful in *Wonder Boys*. I thought he was great in *Cider House Rules*. I thought they were taking a huge risk in putting him in [*Spider-Man*].

And I really appreciated what [producer] Laura Ziskin and [director] Sam Raimi have done with that picture. I was so disappointed in the second and third installments of *Batman* because they were just so dark and sinister and I didn't want my kid to see them. You know, I just walked out depressed. And in this one: *superheroes!* We need superheroes in life today. We really do. And so much of that was Tobey Maguire bringing the humanity into the character. Really. He's totally unique. He's in a category unto himself. And is really going to be a big star depending on what he picks next. Very interesting. I don't think five years ago *any* of us could have foreseen that Tobey Maguire would be Spider-Man and would open with $114 million, even though it *was* in thirty-six hundred theaters, which is setting a new record.

Notice how her answer buzzed superficially around the topic we'd been discussing—the emotional qualities of encountering and admiring a star—then veered to the politics of the movie's production, took a stab at sociology ("We need superheroes"), and finally, like a heat-seeking missile, headed straight for the economic significance of who Tobey Maguire is.

Something similar happened when, trying to get a sense of her personal tastes, I asked, "What have you been reading lately?"

I'm reading, I think it's number nine on the paperback bestseller list. It's Coben's *Tell No One*. And it's very suspenseful. And I just finished reading, oh my gosh, I'm a great, uh, I've read almost everything Tom Clancy, Robert Ludlum, have written. And what did I just finish the other night?

Not Grisham's latest. If you ask me what was on last night's show, because I've been promoting tonight's show all morning, I can't even begin to tell you what was our lead story last night. Um. I don't know. But I'm looking forward to the new *Harry Potter* coming out. Is it due out in July? I think it was originally supposed to but I don't think it is now. But I'm, um, I had the great pleasure of meeting Robert Ludlum. Had him over for dinner at our place in Montana a couple of years ago and of course he died last year. But I had read *everything* that he had done. So I'm excited about *The Bourne Identity* coming to the big screen. And I hear it's pretty good. And of course *The Sum of All Fears*. I mean, get two blockbuster novels coming out with the two buddies Matt Damon and Ben Affleck, I think that's an interesting transition in competition.

That was her verbatim answer, without any interruptions or follow-ups, and after reading it dozens of times, I still think it's a mesmerizing speech. At the beginning she rolled her eyes and screwed up her nose, momentarily unable to recall the title of the book she was reading but sure of its place on the best-seller list. Then, when she couldn't remember the second most recent book she'd read, she just started naming writers—big, famous, best-selling writers. Then, self-conscious, she tried to explain why she'd stumbled remembering the name of the book that she was reading: because she is crushingly overloaded with information—it's not even seven A.M., for crying out loud, and she's already been "on" for two hours, promoting tonight's show while I've been drilling her with questions, and the crush won't end until today's taping is done (at which point the publicist Sandy Brokaw will shake his head and say to me, "I don't know how they do it every single day. They've always got the gun to their heads"), and then it's time to start prepping for tomorrow. How can you possibly remember anything when you're working at that pace?

She kept on trying to answer the question, or at least to offer some related information that might be helpful or interesting, words like moths batting their wings against a screen door. The answer morphs into an exercise in association: news about a brand name, a memory of a limited-edition experience of a brand-name person ("of course he died last year"), and in the end the words swirl inexorably back to the movies, or really, to the movie stars, the buddies Matt and Ben, raising a question—*what's it like for them to be competing now?*—that, to your surprise, triggers a faint pang of real emotion, a mix of sympathy and schadenfreude, because you're both sad and eager to think of it: buddies competing like racehorses to see who's the best, the most popular, which one the world's going to crown the winner.

When one of the deejays asked Mary to record a promo for his show, *Hot Hollywood Gossip*, she said politely, "Oh, I just don't like the word *gossip*. How about 'Hot Hollywood Talk'?" Well, he explained awkwardly, *Hot Hollywood Gossip* was the title of his show. She tightened her lips, then said, yes, she'd be happy to give him the promo.

Later Mary explained to me that she doesn't like to be associated with the word *gossip* because gossip plays fast and loose with the truth. "If we hadn't based this show on factual information, I don't think we'd be around today.

142

We would have been mired in lawsuits." I asked if it had been hard, in the beginning, to toe that line.

"A few years ago, one of the slogans to promote the show became 'We give good gossip.' It was on billboards around the city. And I didn't know about it until I saw it up there. And I said"—here, she put on a big, histrionic voice—"'Oh my *gosh*, all these years we fought against the word, and here it is on a billboard!'" Then her voice dropped low and moved fast: "It didn't last long. It was so counterproductive to what we've tried to establish all these years." More recently, the show's billboard slogan has been "Not just at the scene, part of it."

In addition to her moral objection to gossip, Mary may be averse to it because it's simply a different way of talking about stars than she and *ET* originally chose. In the days of Hedda and Louella and *Confidential* magazine, Hollywood journalists trafficked in gossip because gossip is personal, and American fans understood their relationships to stars in more purely personal terms. *Entertainment Tonight* helped create and satisfy public demand for a different but complementary kind of information, about the business of entertainment, and this helped to change the experience of fandom. More fans came to understand (albeit in a flickering and compartmentalized way) that a movie star's job is not only to be her glorious self, but, more fundamentally, to make money.

ET has always also slaked the public's thirst for details of stars' personal lives. But when I asked Mary why she thinks fans are interested in these things, her answer was again framed in economic terms and could be summarized as, *It's a fun way for people to channel their class envy.*

Q: Why do fans love stars? Why do people watch *Entertainment Tonight*?

A: Because everybody fantasizes about having the success and having the lifestyle that they want to imagine these stars have. It may sound a little trite, but we don't have royalty, so we can't fantasize about being royalty in this country. But we fantasize about being movie stars and television stars and music stars. And in many respects it's very, very glamorous. But behind all the glamour is a lot of hard work. And a lot of heartache. And people know that, too. But it's living vicariously.

Q: Are those fantasies good for people?

A: Oh, I think so. Absolutely. Because it removes you from what may seem to be the humdrum everyday way of life that you want to imagine yourself away from.

Q: Is that bad for people, in any way?

A: People carry it to the extreme, sure. And you get extreme fans. But no. I think it's kind of a nice form of escapism.

Here she brightened and, coming back on point, said, "And you know what? You also have to look at the bottom-line dollar. People in this country spend a lot of money on amusement, entertainment. Billions and billions and billions of dollars. Every year."

In this regard, *ET*, from its conception, has been almost perfectly aligned with the Hollywood establishment's view of stars and fans as cash cows, a sympathy that surely helped cinch Mary Hart's extraordinary success. A couple of months after I interviewed Mary, I met her boss, Joel Berman, the president of Paramount Worldwide Television Distribution, at a promotional event for *Dr. Phil*. Before we watched Dr. Phil's presentation ("There are two kinds of people in the world: the ones that *get it*, and the ones that don't"), I asked whether there were any shows in Paramount's fall production schedule that he was particularly excited about, anything he really loved.

"I've been in this business a long time. And what I like and what I support is what's going to make me a lot of money," he said, his tone informative, not deadpan. "You know, wave the flag, drink the Kool-Aid. Whatever it is, I'll do it."

After a quick tour of the fact-checking and design offices and the newsroom (where, in a scene straight out of *Fahrenheit 451*, everyone had stopped work to whoop and cheer for a car chase that was being broadcast on a big-screen TV—I asked one person what was happening, and she said, "It's *real* life. Sadly"), I watched Mary tape her voice-overs of intros and outros (the narration that accompanies factoids and previews that run just before and after commercial breaks). She put on a different pair of spectacles, entered a brown-walled, soundproof booth whose glass window was marked with fingerprints, and began recording: "Three . . . Two . . . One . . . Celebrating a birthday today . . . Darren McGavin turns eighty."

When she's working, Mary Hart's voice brims with forcefulness that her natural speaking voice lacks, almost as if the voice were a vehicle she's riding: one syllable surging like a speedboat, the next popping like a pogo stick. She vigilantly corrected semantic errors in the text, as when a bit about a *Laverne & Shirley* retrospective had the stars of that show "resuming their roles," and Mary explained to the line's wayward author, "If you're *resuming*, you're just picking up where you left off. What they're doing is *reprising*." (She turned to me and said, "I'm still an English teacher!")

Then, after hair and makeup, she taped the day's show. This was boring, which may sound like a strange thing to say about a show splashed with swirling graphics and punctuated by lightning and thunder sound effects, but most of the bells and whistles are inserted in the control room. And it's hard to get a coherent sense of the program from visiting the set, because the segments are shot out of sequence, and then, as one of the producers explained, "edited into time on the computer" before the finished product is beamed to stations via satellite in early afternoon.

Between takes, there was some chitchat. Bob Goen said, "Fran Drescher seems different," and Mary said, "She got over herself." Sandy the publicist walked over to me and said, "I was thinking, about John Tesh. It's like he was never here." I asked what that meant, and he said, "Just that. It's like he was never here." On the stage, Bob Goen kept flubbing a line that summarized the day's headlines and finally made a joke of the whole thing: "*All* these stories! Everybody's cancer! And babies!"

Bob's joke helps describe a shift in the character of *Entertainment Tonight* that's taken place during the past few years, a swing away from the straight news reporting that was *ET*'s original interest, and toward the sensationalism and gossip that Mary Hart dislikes. The shift is explained, in part, by the sensibilities of executive producer Linda Bell Blue, who came to *ET* from *Hard Copy*, Paramount's aggressive tabloid show, which was canceled in 1999. Under her influence, *ET* broadened its definition of entertainment to include stories like society murder trials and the Bush twins' drinking habits. A typical broadcast under Linda's watch led with the headline "Hollywood reacts to the discovery of Chandra Levy's body." (Reba McEntire said, "I feel for the parents.")

Rob Silverstein, the executive producer of *Access Hollywood*, said, "There are a lot of people who have known Mary Hart for years who can't believe what has happened to that show, can't believe the kinds of stories that are coming out of her mouth now."

When I asked Mary about the shift, she said, "All television is more sensationalistic now, and, yes, we along with it. The news makes scandal-tainted people into celebrities, and we have always covered celebrities."

It's true that *ET* has ceded its old turf of straight news reporting about the business of Hollywood. (To the extent that any entertainment show does this now, it's *Access Hollywood*.) But with the rise of reality television, *ET*, *Access Hollywood*, and every other Hollywood news show has started covering the shady dealings of would-be business tycoons, the heedless plastic surgeries of people who want to look like celebrities, and the unrepentant adultery of models stranded on desert islands. In a short time, reality TV has not only changed the relationship between civilians and celebrities; it's made a corresponding change in the relationship between gossip and entertainment.

Although publicity stunts have always been handy tools

for star-making, and the personal lives of stars have always been a central aspect of their allure, until recently it was possible to distinguish gossiping about famous people from enjoying their work. (My mother probably knew every episode of *Little House on the Prairie*, but she had no idea who Michael Landon ever dated.)

In reality shows, entertainment and gossip have merged. The shows are populated almost entirely by people who do the sorts of things on camera (lie, cheat, have nose jobs and group sex, tell their parents to fuck off) that have always been gossip's favorite topics, because almost no one, until recently, would admit to doing them—let alone perform them in public. Reality TV succeeds because its fans like to watch these taboos being broken, and it makes the stuff of gossip into more than a prop for the entertainment business. In television, gossip has become the coin of the realm. And because television is such a convenient and easy source of everyday entertainment, the way that fans relate to TV stars shapes our whole view of starworld.

In a sense, when Mary Hart reads tabloid headlines about reality stars today, she hasn't really strayed so far from reading the box office grosses way back when. The evolution of *Entertainment Tonight* helps to show that even as fans have become a bit more knowledgeable about the business of entertainment, their appetite for personal details about the world of celebrities has grown more ravenous. This shouldn't be surprising to anyone, though. It takes a lot of time and effort—and most of all, repetition of the same old stupid mistakes—for knowledge to yield anything like enlightenment. How many times have you fallen for somebody who's clearly bad for you?

*   *   *

Entertainment Tonight became a sensation for complicated reasons, and the Mr. Rogers appeal of Mary Hart has many layers, but her surface appeal is by far the most important, and that surface has not changed. Today, whenever people see her—"everywhere, at any time," she says—they sing the *ET* theme song, but she said she doesn't think of herself as a star. "I see myself as being successful, but a star? I don't really like that term, about me."

I understand that she needs to say this kind of thing, that maintaining the illusion that she's just plain Mary is the only way to keep her place in the shark pool, which is the only way for just plain Mary to exist; and I believe that the world of entertainment is a better place for having her. She's being disingenuous, nonetheless. At another point in the conversation, she said that she doesn't send autographed pictures through the mail anymore because "the FBI doesn't want you to sign them, because there are these strange fans." She refused to talk about her own experience with a stalker several years ago, and when I asked how she came in contact with the FBI, she said, "I'm talking in general, their recommendation to celebrities."

After meeting Mary Hart, I can never be a fan again in quite the same way. I still believe that she's a decent person. I also understand more clearly that she's compromised, a calculating cog in a brutal industry. Like everyone who succeeds in this business, she has internalized the entertainment industry's way of treating people—both the famous and the fans—as just the means of making money. But it would be a mistake to accuse her of bad face, because she doesn't hide her compromises. Her audience just chooses not to notice, or not to be bothered by them.

As long as Mary Hart hosts *Entertainment Tonight*, I'm sure I'll still tune in from time to time, for the same reason most of her audience does. Her cheerfulness has an element of real warmth that the rest of TV's entertainment journalists lack, and it functions in some small way, whether she means it to or not, as a protest against the brutality of her business. It's like an ember of the hope and fantasy that drove her fourteen-year-old self to talk her way backstage at that Beatles concert. For me, Mary Hart always offers a little taste of that cocktail of reassurance and humiliation that hooked me as a teenager—a poison that stunted my growth, to be sure, but also a balm that got me through the days until I learned that my life counts just as much as any star's.

In the day I spent with Mary Hart, she may have been most revealing about her experience as a fan, and the trade-offs she's made to become famous, when we talked about her childhood dream of being both Wendy and Peter Pan. It was the moment when I liked her best, and when she made me saddest. She said, "I swear, until I was sixteen, I thought I could fly. I dreamed about it. My dreams were so vivid. I really thought at times I could fly. It's bizarre. I suppose I'd still like to be Peter Pan and Wendy both. When I finally had my opportunity, when I was asked to play Peter Pan in Providence at a very, very well-known theater there, I couldn't do it because I couldn't get enough time off."

She did not sound the least bit disappointed. She was smiling, as if knowing that someone had imagined her in that role were pleasing enough.

I asked if she still has flying dreams today. Still smiling, she said, "No, I don't."

*   *   *

A couple of weeks after I interviewed Mary, I received a wildly peppy message on my voice mail: "Hi, Michael, this is Manfred Westphal from Paramount Television. I'm vice president of media relations for Paramount Domestic Television, and I'm calling you regarding your wonderful story that you're writing for Mary Hart—our *Entertainment Tonight* number one girl, you might say."

Because I was still ignorant of the way publicity works, I was puzzled by the call. How did the elaborately titled Manfred know about the "wonderful story" I was writing "for" Mary Hart? I soon learned that, in addition to having personal publicists (the Brokaw twins) and publicists for *Entertainment Tonight* (two of which I was dealing with), Mary Hart, like any star, also has a battery of other studio publicists—and that all of them confer and try to massage a journalist during the production of a story. (After the profile was published, I met two more Paramount publicists—making a total of seven publicists in all—who claimed to have "worked on" the piece.)

For every reporter spying from his perch atop the Wall of Fame, there's a battalion of publicists whose job is to guard that Wall, making sure the reporter keeps his distance. Their defense tactics, particularly those of personal publicists, are aggressive and numerous. If you ask for a face-to-face interview, they try to make it happen by phone. If you ask for forty-five minutes, they counteroffer you fifteen. They wait to schedule until the last minute, then reschedule at least twice, often on a few hours' notice. They ignore requests for background material because they want to keep you empty-headed, so as to discourage hard questions. The most powerful publicists, like Pat Kingsley (who represented Tom Cruise for years), have been known to force journalists to sign contracts that stipulate precisely what questions may be asked, and where and how any material from an interview is used. Once the interview is done, publicists like to tell you what a lucky duck you are to have scored such amazing access to a star. They call frequently, asking if your story will be "positive." (Want to schedule a follow-up chat? "I think she's in St. Bart's.") If, after all this battering, you write a single unflattering word about a publicist's client, she will blackball you from her company's client list until hell freezes over (or at least until you get assigned a cover story she wants so bad that, to get it, she would fry her child tempura).

In Hollywood, publicists guard every door. They have the key to every lock. In *The Matrix*, Morpheus uses those same phrases to describe the characters called Agents—square-jawed guys in black suits. Most publicists, who dress impeccably and without a trace of personal style, are equally difficult to distinguish from one another.

Morpheus also describes Agents as "sentient programs" designed to guard the false world of appearances that fools human beings into believing that they're fully alive. Agents may take any form—voluptuous siren, kindly old man—but when the Matrix is threatened, they shed those identities and emerge in their anonymous, black-suited battle garb.

Similarly, publicists are single-mindedly devoted to maintaining a seamless public image for their clients, the kind of image that makes fans believe that Hollywood truly is the Technicolor world. Any perceived threat to that image triggers a publicist's irrational and absolute fight mechanism. When I was assigned a story about M., a young European actress making her American film debut, I asked to follow her through her first press junket, to observe her interactions with the media here and describe her experience of culture clash. I called the film's studio publicist, who is one of my closest friends in L.A.

He absolutely refused—"Nothing behind-the-scenes. Ever"—in a steely tone of voice that I barely recognized as his.

I said, "You know me. You know that I'm not out to embarrass anyone. I think M. is great. Why don't you think about it and call me back later?"

"No. What if she gets tired? What if a journalist asks a stupid question and she rolls her eyes? You'd see it, and you'd have every right to report it. There is no benefit ever to be gained from a story that shows what goes on behind the curtain. It's not that I don't trust you. It's that I don't trust anybody."

Almost without exception, when I ask publicists about their experiences with fans, they respond with sneering disdain. Many describe fans as "retarded." "Parasites" is another word I hear a lot, and implied leech or vampire metaphors are common: "They have no life, and so they try to suck the life from stars." Several have volunteered, "I have nothing in common with them," without my having asked if they did.

It's not hard to figure out where this contempt comes from. When one person views another with such scorn, it's usually because he sees in the other some quality of his own that he hates. Midway through an ahi salad or, for the tougher nuts, after a drink or three, they make some sweet confessions:

"When I moved to California, I literally fainted when I got off the plane because I was breathing air in the same state that Shaun Cassidy was breathing air."

"I *was* Anthony Michael Hall in *Sixteen Candles*. I wore his clothes, I had braces, I talked like him. I had the poster framed in my room. People always told me that I looked like him, and it made me so happy."

"This is a picture of me and my best friend in grade school. We made those *Star Trek* costumes ourselves. And now LeVar Burton just drops by my office sometimes, and I still have to pinch myself. I love my life."

"If you talk to Paul McCartney, *tell him I want to marry him!*"

What's difficult is imagining how a person could do a publicist's job *without* being a fan. They live to defend the shiny public image of their stars, to be close to the famous and covet their secrets. Personal publicists, in particular, are always on call and are often treated shabbily. Many stars think nothing of ringing them at night or on weekends, or asking them to run such publicity-related errands as picking up the laundry. In return for slavish devotion, publicists sometimes get to enjoy the lifestyle of the stars—five-star hotels, Michelin's favorite restaurants, first-class flights—in that rarefied world where "queue" is just a letter in the alphabet. "I can never do anything else for work," one publicist told me. "Sometimes they treat me like shit, but then we go on some trip and I'm treated like royalty. I'm addicted to a life that I will never be able to afford."

Publicists, as a group, are the nakedest emperors in town. They know that they are living on borrowed prestige, so any apparent threat to their power is cause for violent alarm. Although quite a few publicists are perfectly civil—and some of them are sterling—as a group they are known as foulmouthed, short-fused status-mongers. (One network executive said that his company's top publicist "uses *fuck* as an *article*.") That reputation creates a vicious circle: journalists expect publicists to be nasty, and so nastiness is what we get. "People are getting meaner and meaner, and it makes me get meaner and meaner, too," one studio publicist told me. The result is a constant state of battle-readiness in which practically everyone on either side of the Wall of Fame seems to lose track of who they are or what drew them to these jobs in the first place.

When I profiled Kelsey Grammer for the *New York Times*, I went back to Paramount to the set of *Frasier*, where I spent a few days watching Kelsey work, and he told me to return on the day when Katie Couric was to interview him on set for *Dateline*. After that, Kelsey said, we would all go to his house in Malibu, where Katie Couric would interview him first, and then I would interview him. L., the Paramount publicist for the show, agreed to this plan, so I showed up on the appointed morning ready to wait.

I had already done a lot of waiting while arranging this story. R., another Paramount publicist, had approached me with the offer to profile Kelsey; when I pitched it to the *Times* and got assigned, I requested background materials (videotapes of the show, old articles about the actor) from L. and had to follow up five times before I received anything at all from her. After waiting weeks for the publicist to schedule the interview with Kelsey, I received a strange call from R., who told me she was glad I'd worked things out with B., Kelsey's personal publicist, and were we good to go?

I'd never heard *of* B., much less *from* him, and when I said so, R. flew off the handle: "The lying sack of shit. I'll tell you about B. Fucking useless. Lazy. All he wants to do is hang out with celebrities. Fucking, fucking *useless*. I'll get on it."

Several phone calls later, each of which featured more embroidery on R.'s colorful assessment of B., we were all set.

On the day I'd been invited to visit Malibu, I hung out for rehearsal, then watched Katie Couric interview the show's whole cast on set. Afterward, Katie and I were introduced by L., the publicist, and Katie asked if I'd seen her interview with the plagiarist Jayson Blair (I hadn't) and told me how "proud" she was of it. Then Katie and I both sat on the furniture in Frasier's living room and made calls on our cell phones. In a few minutes, she came over to me and asked, "Were you just listening in on my conversation?"

"No," I said. "Were you just listening in on mine?"

She forced a laugh, but I sensed suspicion or hostility, and I wanted to defuse it. I stood up from Frasier's dad's ratty Barcalounger and said, "This is the most comfortable chair ever. You should try it."

She reluctantly sat down in the chair and patted the arms. "It's nice," she said, but she wasn't warming up.

Later, I wondered why I chose that particular strategy of trying to make nice with Katie Couric. I could have said anything, and what I said was, *Check out this chair—*

which, on the set of *Frasier*, was the same as saying, *Spend a minute playing the fan with me*. What makes this even stranger is that I'm not a particular fan of *Frasier*—it's a funny show, but Kelsey Grammer doesn't do anything to quicken my pulse. Even so, I must have felt on some level that the easiest way to overcome the tension with Katie was to get ourselves out of the way and enter, for a moment, the experience of enjoying this famous place together.

"We could get somebody to take your picture in it," I offered. "Good souvenir." Instantly, I knew that I'd said something wrong.

"Oh, no, that's okay. That won't be necessary," she said, and walked away.

Rehearsal dragged on for a couple more hours, and then Kelsey's personal publicist, B., came over to tell me, "You won't be able to come to Malibu today, because L. forgot that she'd promised an exclusive to Katie."

Steamed, I went over to the Paramount publicity office to ask R. what was going on. This runaround was maddeningly consistent with the publicists' behavior throughout the reporting of this story. I had put up with their garbage without a peep until now. But this was cause for peeping. "L. knew I was coming for the trip to Malibu. Now she claims she 'forgot' it was an exclusive for Katie? It doesn't square. What happened here?"

"When Katie Couric found out there was a reporter from the *New York Times*, she said she didn't want you around." She stared at me.

"So you're just spiking me, end of story?"

"What?" she asked, raising her voice to put me in my

place. "Should I have told Katie Couric to fuck off?" She
chomped onto "fuck" like it was a celery stick.

"I guess you've got no compunction about telling the
New York Times to fuck off." I'm usually not that quick
on my feet, and I'd never fought with a publicist like this
before. I wondered where that line had come from.

Just like in a movie, she pressed a button on her desk and
her office door swung shut.

She raised her voice a little more: "You calm down and
sit your butt right there."

"You stop ordering me around in that patronizing voice,
and I will."

Showdown. Deep breaths. She said, "Okay. Look. I'm
pregnant. I'm *extremely* hormonal. I'm *crazed*. And do
you have any idea how much access you've had? It is
amazing. Amazing. How much access you've had."

"Yes," I said, biting it. "You've been very generous."

A beat. A ray of light: "Thank you. What can we do to
solve this?"

We worked it out—Katie got an exclusive on the Malibu
visit; I got an exclusive visit to his new house in the
Hollywood Hills—and I drove home feeling filthy from
the fight.

The word *fuck* does not usually come to mind, much less
roll off my tongue, in professional conversation, and I kind
of hated that I'd so automatically and willingly been
dragged down to R.'s level. I felt less than human, but
also weirdly full of power. I was pumped with adrenaline,
hyperalert, just shy of shaky.

Later, I realized, this physical sensation was a little bit
like being starstruck. And when I figured this out, I
wondered whether journalists and publicists and practi-

cally everyone else in Hollywood actually seek out these clashes because, on some deep level, they remind us of the adrenaline rush of loving stars that was the reason we got into this business to begin with. These foulmouthed, short-fused fights happen constantly in the entertainment industry, and they're almost always somehow related to playing with other people's fame.

A Hollywood pissing match feels a lot like meeting a star you admire. You feel bigger and more powerful than your normal self while the encounter lasts. Then it ends, and you're deflated. What seemed to be self-assertion has actually reduced you. Yet what you feel in your body—this sense of power, this addictive adrenaline rush—overwhelms what you know in your brain. So pretty soon, you find it's happening again.

L. called me a few days later. Without apologizing for, or even explaining, the Katie Couric snafu, she said, "I just want you to know that that whole day you were here, when Katie was here, was off-the-record."

A little surge in my stomach. Carefully I said, "We both know how this works. Nothing's off-the-record unless you tell me beforehand that it's off-the-record."

"Are you gonna fuck me?" she snapped.

If I had to have these conversations, I figured, I might as well enjoy them just a little bit.

"Why in the world," I asked slowly, "would I want to fuck you?"

There are a few places where the publicists' stranglehold on access to celebrities is loosened. The Sundance Film Festival in Park City, Utah, is known as one of the freest mixers of stars, fans, journalists, and studio executives (although that's changing as the event grows more popular and commercial). As a result, most publicists don't like Sundance. "You should see the fans there! It's awful," one told me. "These *nobodies*, demanding to get into the parties. They don't even *know* that they're nobodies. And the clients are all, *whatever*, talking to everybody, and you can't control them at all."

I booked my ticket immediately.

Sundance was like old home week. Outside one screening I saw Ben, the autograph collector-cum-paparazzi ("Chasing them down's a little easier here because the barrel's smaller. But it's still the same basic formula"). He was hanging out with a few of the autograph collectors I knew from L.A., including one that I'd met two years prior, Bart, a lanky, handsome guy who told me that at age twenty-three he had "retired" from collecting. "I just got sick of chasing people. I was good, you know? I met everyone I wanted to meet. But for most of these guys it's an addiction. It all comes down to, when you die, you can't take the autographs with you. There's more important things in life." So what was he doing here now? "I moved to Utah. It's fun just to come up and hang out for a couple of days. But no autographs anymore. I'm just standing around."

Everywhere I went, there were stars. I hung out with Tilda Swinton at a concert in a little club and we howled along with the imaginary language of Sigur Rós. I ran into Val Kilmer and Daryl Hannah outside a restaurant one night and introduced myself and told them about my book. "Are you the Michael Gross who dated my sister?" she asked. I said no, but did she have a brother? She hugged me and said, "I love you!" and Val gave me a high five, and just like that, they took me back to the house where they were staying to talk for a while.

Val said, "When I was young, I tried to act according to certain principles. You know, not sign autographs because somebody might sell it or get an inflated idea of your worth. But it's like, do you give every bum on the street money, or do you not give any of them anything just because somebody's gonna go buy crack with it?" So he started signing autographs again. "I realized you can't control what people do, what comes of your actions. It's not in your power."

My week at Sundance was the first time I'd interacted with celebrities in a context that was not designed by publicists to provide constant reminders of how lucky I was to be interacting with celebrities. I'd only been in Park City for a few hours when I found myself playing buddy to a famous actor for the first time in my life. To meet this guy, I had to make a clear choice to hurt another person's feelings, to ignore my roots for the sake of my dreams. What happened next felt kind of like a breakthrough, a more authentic connection than my previous interviews with stars, even though in the end I realized I was really just soaking in the same old swill.

My first night at Sundance, at a party in a tent at the foot of Park City's ski lift, I met a pretty brunette with deep brown eyes who said, "I think I've met you before."

People say this to me a lot, so I've developed a flow chart of stock responses to the remark and its follow-ups. "I'm a type," I said.

"No, really. Do you look like someone famous?"

"People say I look like Sean Hayes."

"Sort of, but no. Who else?"

"When men are very drunk and want to sleep with me, they say I look like a young Marky Mark."

"That's funny! You're gay?"

Nice to meet you, moving on . . .

But she followed me. "Hey! Where did you grow up?"

"Illinois."

Eyes bigger: *"Where?"*

Pay dirt. Her name is Emily, and she is from Jacksonville, Illinois, the medium-size town of which my hometown is a satellite. We had met, we were both sure, but we couldn't remember how. And then she used a magic word that nearly blew my mind:

"I was a J'ette."

When I was in high school, the J'ettes—pronounced "jay-*ette*," unless you're in Paris—the Jacksonville High School pom-pom squad, were the gold standard of young womanhood in central Illinois. My friends and I would skip our own high school basketball games on the weekends and go to Jacksonville's instead, just so we could watch the J'ettes' halftime routines.

After the Jacksonville ball games, my friends and I would hang out in the parking lot at Hardee's, where we met and became reasonably friendly with a few girls who knew the J'ettes, who eventually introduced us to the J'ettes themselves, who on subsequent occasions would sometimes remember our names.

(One winter we even met the queen of the squad, Heather, the daughter of an optometrist, who had golden hair and drove a white VW Cabriolet convertible with a vanity plate that said BUNNY 94. A few weeks after meeting her I stomped "I ♥ U" in the snow in the yard beneath her bedroom window, then called to reveal the author's identity. Trying to place me, she asked, "What kind of car do you drive?" and the conversation ended shortly after I answered, "A '72 Delta 88." When I heard that Heather was in *Playboy* a few years ago, I bought the magazine and was pleased to find myself unmoved.)

Meeting Emily at Sundance was the first time since leaving Winchester that I had run into a person from my growing-up years. With Fran Drescher standing ten feet away, we played the name game, and I was remembering faces and sounds of voices that I hadn't thought of in ten years. We sat down on a sofa and talked for a long time, tracing our separate paths to L.A., and she told me about her place in the Valley and how hard it is to be an actress. There was huge relief in this meeting, because finally I wasn't the only person from where I come from who'd gone to where I'd gone. And yet, as we talked more, I started to feel uncomfortable, too. She asked questions like "Why do you think we got out?" and "Did you ever dream you'd be at a party like this?" and "Can you believe running into each other here?" in a voice that was too bright, eager, and earnest. Yes, I could believe it. Couldn't she?

There was another party down the street, for *Spun*, a movie about speed freaks directed by Jonas Akerlund, who has directed music videos for Madonna. I told Emily that I was going to this party and asked if she'd like to come along, although I wasn't sure whether they'd let me bring a guest. Walking to the party, she held on to my arm and said, "All the J'ettes always thought you were so cute." I knew she was flattering me, but I was still kind of thrilled that she would bother.

The crowd outside the party was ten deep, everyone hollering and jostling to get the bouncer's attention. As I held Emily's hand to keep from being separated in the crowd, we nudged through, I gave my name, and they let us in. Emily said, "I can't believe we got in!"

Inside the party, the crowd clustered around another bouncer at the roped-off stairway to the upstairs VIP room. We nudged through again and I gave my name. "We're over fire code," he said. "I can't let anybody else in for a few minutes."

We stood back for a few minutes, during which the bouncer unhitched the velvet rope to let in about a dozen people.

"Is the fire code on a sliding scale?" I asked, trying ineffectively to mask hostility with humor.

"You're not getting up," he said. "Only celebrities and people who worked on the film."

I felt like I was in high school again. The stratification of the cool people and the dorks. I knew the whole scene was obnoxious, and on principle I wanted to go home right then. But I told myself that the reason I'd come to Sundance was to run exactly the gauntlet represented by that stairway, and I knew that I could go up there if I just got a little bit creative.

Then I looked at Emily and imagined taking her upstairs and trying to do interviews and having her tell everybody how she couldn't believe we got in.

I went to find my PR contact, who then walked me to the bouncer and whispered something in his ear. He scowled and looked away and unhitched the rope, and the publicist went ahead of me as I started up the stairs, still holding Emily's hand. I felt the bouncer's forearm chop down on our two hands and I let go. I turned my head to see him say, "You only," then turned to see Emily behind the rope, looking pleadingly, and probably angrily, up at me. My decision was so unthinking it felt programmed. I mouthed, "Sor-ry," and looked away before I could register her reaction. I had given her my cell phone number earlier that night and we had promised that we would have dinner when we got back to L.A., but, needless to say, she hasn't called.

"Who do you want to talk to?" the publicist asked. The air was thick like in a locker room.
"Who have you got?" I asked.
"Mena Suvari."
Um, perfect.

So *American Beauty*'s ideal pom-pom girl and I sat under a ficus tree next to a fireplace with a line of red Lava lamps and Jonathan Adler vases on the mantel, and we yelled at each other over the music. She said, "I saw Pauly Shore tonight!" but the people she'd met at Sundance who'd made her feel most starstruck were Adrien Brody and Daniel Day-Lewis. "I got all weird. They think I'm retards." She put on a retard face, stuck out her lip, and made a *luh-wuh-luh* sound. "I hate being tacky like that. And I'm sure they didn't know who the fuck I was. I'm, like, all drooling. It's so embarrassing when you can't think of anything to say and you're just, like, drooling." I said that I was surprised she felt that way, and she said, "Don't you feel like that sometimes? And afterwards you're all, criticizing yourself?"

She said that when she's recognized in public, she doesn't immediately connect the response to her celebrity. "People look at me and my reaction is always like, 'Get out of my face.' I never think they know who I am. I don't want to. I never want to think like that."

I said that I found that a little hard to believe. I asked her what it would take to make her realize that strangers were staring at her because they'd seen her in movies.

She didn't answer the question directly. Instead, she denied an accusation that I hadn't made: "I'm honestly no different from so many people. I'm just as much of a dork. What will change that? Nothing. It's not about, I think I'm *more* than anybody else. I just, this is just—it's what I *do*."

The publicist came back and asked if I wanted to talk to Mickey Rourke. (Publicists always say "talk to," they never say "talk with.") Mickey, who looked like he had been dragged behind a truck for fourteen miles, said hi and immediately started talking about how uncool the party was—"In this room there's very little talent"—but I found him weirdly charming anyway. He wanted you to have a good time, and he wanted to give you a break from the bullshit posing at this party, where everybody looked like they were trying out for one of Jonas's music videos.

He said that no one had ever made him feel starstruck, but that he admires Bob Dylan most, of all the people he's worked with. "Bob is a legend. The way he carries himself. Maintains his privacy. He's done the hardest thing that anybody can do. I definitely think he'll go to heaven, you know. And I'd like to be right behind him. It's hard to stay here, you know. Bob stayed here, man. He survived." While Mickey was saying this, he was feeling up a black woman with cornrows who later told me her name was Tia. "Sorry I'm grabbing ass while I'm talking to you." I said that was okay.

Regarding his own relationships with fans, Mickey said, "I never really dealt with them a lot. I never knew anybody would like me for anything I did. I know I'm good at what I do. But it ends right there. It's like a dog that's been kicked in the ass when it was young. You're hurt. You're sort of okay deep down, but not really. And nothing can touch that." He turned to Tia and asked, "That vodka?" She nodded. He took the glass, poured the drink down the front of his jeans, swiveled his hips, and said, "We're ready to go now."

We hung around for another half hour or so. I talked with Tia, a personal trainer who had worked with Mickey in Miami a few years before. "I am also a model/actress/singer. I'm singing at the Bob Marley Fest. The Bob Marley Fest is the only one in Miami that's run and approved by his family."

I put my notebook in my pocket for a moment, and Mickey grabbed my hand and placed it on Tia's rear end. "Isn't that a great ass?" he said as I pulled my hand back and nodded. Tia giggled a little bit.

Time for a break. I sat down on a sofa and talked with a female bodybuilder-turned-novelist for a few minutes. A man in a white cowboy hat with bright red stripes and a figure 8 on the front, a bright red shirt and bright red jeans, with muttonchop whiskers and smoky glasses, came over and introduced himself as Tia's husband, although Tia was behaving as if no such person existed. Mickey, who was sort of grooving in place with Tia, hollered from a few feet away, "I'll bring her back in the morning!"

The husband said, "I feel terrible. That's my wife. But I feel, like, you grow up with Mickey and you love him like your brother. If your brother is aching, you do whatever you can to help him."

Mickey's agent, David Unger from ICM, came over and gently asked what I would and would not be writing about from this evening. He explained that Mickey was at a tender point in his career, trying to make a comeback. He tried to sell me a few little spin phrases on Mickey's behavior, like "He's so bad he's good."

Mickey started licking Tia's face and people took pictures. "I'll fill up your notebook, motherfucker," he told me. "Come on. We're going." We left, with David, Jonas, his girlfriend B (a stylist, who wore dangly earrings with a gigantic silver letter *B*), the female bodybuilder/novelist, and Jason Schwartzman.

Tia and her husband had a private chat at the door downstairs and went off somewhere together.

On the sidewalk outside it was cold and you could see everyone's breath as people started swarming around Mickey. "Hey, Mickey, remember me?" asked one man.

"Where do I know you from?" Mickey asked.

"We used to work out at Gold's together. And I saw you at Starbucks today."

A girl in a white dress with long, straight blond hair said, "Can I tell you that *Barfly* is one of my favorite movies?"

Mickey put his arm around her. "Of course you can. Look at you. So pretty."

She quoted him, throwing one hand up in the air, " 'Drinks for all my friends!' "

Mickey got her number, then whispered in my ear, "David likes blondes. I look out for my friends."

No one said hello to Jason Schwartzman. He was carrying three gift bags from the party, and he kept explaining, "One is for my mother."

Mickey crossed the street to urinate in a doorway. When he returned, in his open black topcoat and open leather shirt, his chest shielded from the weather only by a black T-shirt, a middle-aged woman introduced herself: "I'm from Montana."

Mickey looked at her daughter, who was maybe twelve. "You're pretty. You oughta call me in about ten years."

There were Christmas lights strung across Main Street. We walked down the hill toward another party at the ski lift, and Mickey said, "Hangin' and swingin'. Hangin' and swingin'."

He explained that we were going to a party thrown by Josh Richman, whom he described as "Johnny Depp's best friend, who kind of looks like a drug dealer." It was a long walk. "Are we close? Like, can I spit there?" Mickey asked. David said we were not close. "Man, I can spit far," Mickey said.

Josh Richman's party was in the same tent where I'd met Emily earlier that night, but the space had been transformed. It was aggressively peaceful, like a sheikh's tent in a movie, with soft lighting and pillows on the floor. Walking in, I said, "Where's the opium?" and Floria, an Icelandic stylist who was also with us, said, "Exactly."

Mickey ordered a beer and a shot of tequila for each of us, and although I have a rule against imbibing while reporting, that night I broke it.

He ordered us each another shot of tequila immediately after that, and my penmanship for the next few hours is not very clear.

Most of the evening, he kept approaching women, or women kept approaching him, and he would say things like "You have an amazing body and I have a yard of dick," and they would coo and aah for a few minutes and say they liked his movies, and then they would move on.

At one point, there was a woman in a tight horizontal-striped sweater that made her look like a bumblebee standing next to us. Mickey said, "How old are you?" and she said she was twenty-five.

"Look at this old bitch," he said to me. "If she wasn't so old, I'd take her home." I couldn't tell whether she was pissed off or upset.

He said, "Come on, we're goin' outside," and I said I'd catch up with him in a little bit.

I said to the woman, "He's really, really drunk."

"Who was that guy?" she asked. I told her.

"Mickey O'Rourke?" she said. "I'm gonna kill him. Who the fuck is that?"

In its way, this was an excellent point.

I got a taxi and went to bed, and I had a headache until four the next afternoon. Around that time I remembered that Mickey Rourke was the star of the most terrifying movie I have ever seen. I was seventeen when *Angel Heart* came out. When I got home from that movie, I was so frightened that I literally cried myself to sleep. At the end of the film, Mickey's character, a detective investigating a series of occult murders, understands that the murderer he's after has given his soul to the devil, and the final twist comes when the detective learns that the soul at the heart of the mystery he's been chasing is his own.

I'm not sure whether any description of Mickey's words

and actions could convey the intense lightness he has—really just hangin' and swingin'—not caring a thing about consequences and not thinking about whether the present moment has any logical connection to the one that just passed. It's not how normal people live. It is a mode of careless entitlement that only a star can assume, and it is so intoxicating that, viewed up close, even for a few hours, this kind of existence can seem to be yours, too.

In *Almost Famous*, the fledgling reporter William (alter ego of the film's director, Cameron Crowe, who started writing for *Rolling Stone* when he was a teenager) gets a warning from his mentor, rock critic Lester Bangs: "Friendship is the booze they feed you. They want you to get drunk on feeling like you belong." After my big night with Mickey, I understood this line a little better. The tequila we drank was harsh, but it was nothing compared to the cocktail of reassurance (*I'm cool* because I'm hanging with a movie star) and humiliation (I'm cool *because I'm hanging with a movie star*) that he gave me.

Getting close to a star, even a minor one, can get you smashed if you're not careful. Drunkenness, of course, takes many forms, and the kind I'm talking about is probably best described by some dialogue from the 1938 film *Holiday*, in which the lovesick character Linda Seton (Katharine Hepburn), seeking to forget her troubles, asks her brother Ned (Lew Ayers), "What's it like to get drunk?"

He answers, "Well, to begin with, it brings you to life . . . And after a while you begin to know all about it. You feel, I don't know, *important* . . . And then pretty soon the game starts . . . Swell game, terribly exciting game. You see, you think clear as crystal, but every move, every sentence, is a problem. It gets pretty interesting."

Her voice wavers as she begins to understand: "You get beaten though, don't you?"

"Sure, but that's good, too. Then you don't mind anything, not anything at all. Then you sleep."

"How long can you keep it up?"

"A long while, as long as you last."

As nasty and mendacious as the game of Hollywood publicity and journalism may be, I sometimes think it's the best of all possible systems for this Alice-in-Wonderland world. Maybe journalists are better off with publicists keeping the Wall of Fame well fortified, and maybe fans are better off with journalists airbrushing the images they see here.

Not every celebrity is a badass, but practically all celebrities, even the ones that seem nicest, are narcissistic in some way that's destructive of most of the people they meet face-to-face. Hollywood journalists and publicists are often criticized for magnifying this narcissistic force in our society. They also buffer it, filtering out a lot of the impurities, so that by the time a star's image gets to you, she's refined into something lovelier than she actually is.

There's no question that the distortion practiced by journalists and publicists can have some hurtful effects on fans. I do my best to avoid it, and in an ideal world I would have none of it. But even if the public image of a star like Cary Grant isn't true, it can still serve a good purpose. As David Thomson has asked, "How could anyone 'be' Cary Grant? How can anyone, ever after, not consider the attempt?"

Publicists and journalists who get close to the stars often find themselves behaving in ways that they know to be wrong. To hang out with a star, even if the scene is nasty and tawdry, you might find yourself willing to give up some important things—forget where you come from, behave in ways you know to be unkind. To get into that VIP room, I threw away the chance of a friendship in which Emily and I might have understood some things about each other that no one else in L.A. could. Instead, I spent the evening pretending to be friends with Mickey Rourke, and all I ended up with was a hangover and a story.

4

People Storms

ON MY LAST DAY at Sundance, I saw a group of kids in stocking caps sprinting uphill on the sidewalk of Main Street in Park City: coats unzipped and flapping in the wind, heads little bobbing dots of blue, green, orange, red, and yellow, all hurling forward toward Sean Astin, calling out his hobbit name. "Sam!" they hollered. "Sam! Did you get to keep the feet?"

Inside the clothing store Roots, the official Sundance outfitters, Sean was spotted by a young man who tapped a middle-aged woman on the shoulder and whispered, "Look, Mom, it's—"

"Oh, yeah. I know exactly who that is," she said, striding toward him with a look of relish, before introducing herself as Wendy Krause Goodman, a national sales manager for the clothing company, as she enclosed him in a hug.

She handed Sean a leather tote bag that had been designed for the Jamaican Olympic bobsledding team, and then she painstakingly showed him almost every item of clothing in the store, offering as many of each item as he wanted, for free. Occasionally, they were interrupted by more kids who wanted autographs, and Sean would talk to each one of them until Wendy lured him back with swag.

When Sean saw Cindy Williams (of *Laverne & Shirley*)

entering the store, it was his turn to play the fan. He broke away from Wendy to ask if Cindy would pose for a picture for his Web site, telling her, "I begged to stay up to watch your show."

Cindy blushed and replied, "Oh, your mom is so wonderful," then, after a beat: "Let's all join hands and dance."

Wendy ignored the irony and, with tears in her eyes, congratulated Sean on "making it through your childhood"—an oblique reference to his mother Patty Duke's struggle with manic depression, and the press speculation that once surrounded the identity of Sean's biological father. Wendy said, "You're just wonderful. You're great," as she stuffed a few more shirts into the Jamaican bobsledding bag. "We're open tomorrow if you need any more. And if you need anything in Beverly Hills—"

"What?" he asked, incredulous.

She hesitated a second and then quizzically explained the obvious: "At the Roots store in Beverly Hills . . . ?"

He shook his head and chuckled. "I was gonna say! Do I need anything in Beverly Hills? Um, a Jaguar? A Bentley? Well, there's a house I know that Jimmy Stewart used to have . . ."

Sean didn't really believe that this woman might score him a Bentley, but after having been given more than a thousand dollars' worth of clothing, his joshing was still a trifle strange. Wendy smiled and put her arm around him as he left the store, showing no sign of imagining there'd been anything amiss in their exchange. She just seemed thrilled that, for a few moments, she had been a part of his world.

*   *   *

Sean Astin is nobody's idea of a superstar. But when I watched the crowds of kids flocking to him on Main Street, when I saw the tearful, protective response he elicited from Wendy, and when I spent more time with him in the next several months, I realized that Sean Astin means something to practically everyone—whether for being the son of Patty Duke and John Astin (Gomez on *The Addams Family*), or for his performance in *The Goonies*, or as an archetypal American underdog in *Rudy* (about a kid who realizes his dream of playing football for Notre Dame, despite his lack of athletic ability), or for his best-known role, as Samwise Gamgee, Frodo's hobbit helpmeet in Peter Jackson's *The Lord of the Rings* trilogy.

Sean's best performances offer the same comfort that character actors—the buddies, best friends, and side-kicks—have always given their audiences: that even a person as normal as you could be up there on the screen. Sean's famous parents give him more cachet than most character actors. (Though not enough to save him from a fairly regular string of minor indignities, as when, while campaigning with John Kerry in 2004, the candidate called him "Frodo!" Or the time when he and Elijah Wood were honored with a ninety-cent New Zealand postage stamp, and his last name was spelled "Austin" on the stamp's presentation pack.) Still, even Sean's Hollywood legacy serves less to suggest unique charisma than to provide an extra point of identification allowing fans to imagine themselves into a world that seems a bit grander than our own.

But not *too* much grander. When I first saw *The Fellowship of the Ring*, Sean Astin's performance moved me in a way that Elijah Wood's couldn't—because Sean seemed like a guy I could hang out with, where Elijah's Martian beauty made me think that when no one is looking, he starts talking in buzzes and beeps.

I'm not alone in preferring the reachable stars to the distant ones. Although mystery will always be a potent source of star appeal, the vast majority of movie stars have not been Garbos or Brandos. They've been Christopher Walkens and Holly Hunters. On television, perhaps because the thing is in our living rooms, we prefer stars who are easy to identify with, and who seem to resemble their characters: Camryn Manheim, the fat girl who never lets it get her down; Andy Griffith, the good dad; Shelley Long, the fussy, self-defeating intellectual. In both media, most of our stars are companionable folks: special enough to be worth watching, but not so special that we can't imagine being a part of their world.

But in Hollywood, the social prestige of character actors—even those who star in multibillion-dollar-grossing franchise films—is highly unstable. When I told people here that I was writing about Sean and his fans, many would turn up their noses and ask why I hadn't aimed higher. "He really has fans?" asked one publicist. "Well, I guess he has lost some weight." Another: "But he's B-list." A producer sniffed, "Sean's a character actor. That's all he'll ever be." Clearly uncomfortable with their own condescension, these same people often rushed to qualify their dismissals by calling him a "sweet guy" with a "good heart," and the like.

He evokes this mixture of admiration and disdain in Hollywood because—and this is about the worst thing to be said about the guy—Sean Astin is not cool. The most revered celebrities are the coolest, because coolness covers up the unappealing qualities of neediness and narcissism that, as far as I can tell, almost every star has in common. Performers, and most people with creative jobs in the entertainment industry, are self-obsessed, basically lonely, and fairly desperate for human connection. I have never lived in a community filled with so many smart, interesting people who spend so much time bemoaning the lack of smart, interesting people to hang out with.

Most people who work in the entertainment industry are addicted to their own feelings of alienation, and the products of this industry—driven, always, by a lust for the next cool thing—are in large part efforts to find temporary relief from those feelings. (This is true even of ostensibly moral or high-minded endeavors. When *The Passion of the Christ* opened, one publicist gloated, "Christian is the new gay.") Few are lucky enough to have any secure or consistent association with the world of what's cool; and feelings or fears of exclusion from that world can make for some ethically corrosive social customs. "You got *L.A.'ed*," drawled one buddy of mine during my first months in town, when I began to realize that, in casual Hollywood friendships, social commitments are always subject to cancellation if either party gets invited to hang out with a star.

The kind of friendship I'm talking about takes shape something like this: Upon first meeting a person whose charm, talent, or connections might help brighten our humdrum lives, we wildly overstate our mutual affection. (Take heed of anyone who decides you're "an amazing person" before the appetizers arrive.) There follows a flurry of appointments made and broken, usually because something starry came up. (A screenwriter skipped my dinner party to have drinks with Uma, and I got over it. But then one guy canceled our eighth try at drinks to take a tap-dancing lesson with Jackie Stallone.) Finally, you connect. You remember why you liked each other in the first place. And you actually *do* like each other; neither one's been flaking because you don't care; you've been flaking because you work in the industry of personhood, and you think you'll up your chances for success if you take every opportunity you get to be part of the stars' world—because you believe that if they like you, they can help make your dreams real (and because their mere presence, in the meantime, can at least give some confidence that you're on the way).

You swap stories about the awards shows and premieres and tap-dance lessons that came between you for so long. For dignity's sake, you entertain the chronicles of celebrity socializing with equanimity. You ask some pseudotough, skeptical questions ("Do you really think Amanda Bynes is smart?"), unless the star under discussion is unimpeachably cool, in which case you just reflect your friend's reflected glory back at him—because (even though you don't consciously think this until later, unless you're a monster) maybe this friend's headed for the coolest part of the cool world, and then you, by association, could be that much closer yourself.

In turn, your friend gives the skepticism right back to you—which, because the last time you canceled on him was to go to a party with Sean Astin, might provoke snarky remarks as quoted above, even though, on cross-examination, it turns out that *he actually knows and likes Sean Astin.* No matter. He talks this way for sport, maybe because he had drinks with Sarah Jessica Parker last week, and right now it's much cooler to be part of her world than Sean's. And maybe because the night before, somebody canceled on him to have drinks with Julia Roberts, making him feel about Sarah Jessica Parker the way he's trying to make you feel about Sean tonight. And maybe because he's pissed that, regardless of how many times he has drinks with people who are cooler than Sean Astin, it probably won't ever make *him* cooler than Sean Astin, even though—*madness!*—Sean Astin isn't cool.

But such conscious comparison might unleash the storm of doubts that he keeps silent in his heart. *What if it really doesn't matter who you know, but only what you do? What if all I am, is just a fan, and my dreams of crossing over into starworld are absurd?* He doesn't want to think about those things. He doesn't have to if he looks down on the "B-list" world he builds, put-down by put-down, inside his own head.

In Park City, I introduced myself to Sean as he was leaving the Roots store, and he invited me to hop in the car for the ride back to his hotel. On the way, he processed the interactions he'd just had on Main Street. "I love the moment when people's eyes meet and there's a chance, even just for a nanosecond, to connect, and then you have to decide to go with that connection or turn away from it," he said enthusiastically. "Someone says hello, and you have a split second to negotiate in your mind whether this person is friendly or not, safe or not. It's an orgy of communication and realization in your mind.

"All my life I've wanted to catch people's eyes. When I was little, when we would go somewhere on a plane, my mom and dad would send me up and down the aisles saying, 'Heh-woh! I'm wunning foh may-oh!'" (Patty Duke's autobiography, *Call Me Anna*, alludes to this quality but describes Sean's choice in the matter a bit differently: "I mean, the kid has been running for mayor since he was eighteen months old.")

He asked, "Did you ever do something like that as a kid?"

I told him that my parents always got a big charge out of encouraging precocious little stunts, like the time they sent me around the neighborhood to knock on doors and tell people to vote for Gerald Ford in the race against Jimmy Carter when I was six years old.

"Aren't you glad they did that?" he asked.

"I don't know. Sometimes I think that kind of thing messed me up a little. It encouraged me to be a show-off, always a little bit dissatisfied if I wasn't always the center of attention."

He thought for a minute and said, "I just don't see how that could mess a person up."

We went to his hotel room and spent most of the rest of the afternoon talking. Although I'd never had trouble convincing celebrities to talk about relationships with fans, I'd also never encountered anyone who was quite so thoroughly game. Sean is a thoughtful guy and remarkably candid about the disorienting effects that fans' attention can have on him: "Sometimes when I'm walking down the street, I hear somebody say, 'That's Rudy!' and I'll ask my wife and she says she didn't hear it, and I wonder if it was just in my head."

That night we went to the festival's awards show together. Walking through the hall with him, I saw a world with whole dimensions that my world doesn't have—a world where every move you make is dignified with attention, a world where everyone you meet is poised to shower you with affection, a world where your imperfections and faux pas meet with smiles instead of scowls. Hanging out with Sean, unlike with Mickey Rourke, the only moral compromise I made was indulging some remarks that seemed benignly muddled or puffed up—the kind of thing you let pass in bull sessions, conversation's misfires on the way to reaching insight. Maybe the comparison was flawed, I thought, but that remained to be seen. I liked him. And an hour after I had introduced myself, Sean had fixed me with his eyes and said, with absolute conviction, "I think that you and I are going to be lifelong friends."

Plenty of fans would like to be a part of Sean's world. According to Sean's younger brother MacKenzie Astin, also an actor, a few have taken the desire to delusional extremes. "When we were kids, like thirteen and fifteen, there was one guy from Georgia who would come to the house and write cards saying that he had been sent by God to make beautiful movies with Sean and me in Hawaii and Fiji and Australia. He would put the cards, along with pictures of his kids, in Ziploc bags and leave them on the windshields of the cars or on the front porch." (Another of MacKenzie's favorite family fan stories: "A guy came to the door and my dad answered. The guy said that he had been sent by God to marry my mom. My dad said, 'He sent me first!' And shut the door.") Sean, however, didn't want to talk about his crazy fans. Instead, he told stories about more functional fans who sought out his friendship and described his pleasure at accommodating their desires.

The next time I met with him, about a month later, was at the Beverly Wilshire Hotel, where he'd taken a room for an hour to change clothes before a banquet. His wife, Christine, an Ivory-girl beauty from Indiana whom he'd met in college, was there, too, and his publicist, Gibson, a tiny woman with enormous blue eyes and a blond bob, who kept slipping off to the corner to take calls on her cell phone from someone named Caprice.

When I asked Sean whether he had ever developed close relationships with people who'd first approached him as fans, the first person he named was a lawyer in Boston with whom he had subsequently become friends, and with whom he was developing a film: "He wrote me one of the great fan letters anyone could ever get, on Harvard stationery, which was impressive." (When I later called the guy and asked about the letter, he sounded wounded: "Sean called that a fan letter? I just, I'm a great admirer of his work.")

A few more names rolled off his tongue, and then: "Jeff, my assistant."

Christine said, "He was a fan, as well. Boy, we're really sick," and she, Sean, and Gibson laughed.

Sean said, "They just absorb the energy and put it to good use, that's all. So Jeff wrote a fan letter that was also his résumé—and a description of the meeting he wanted to have in our office—"

Christine explained, "The perfect meeting we weren't giving him."

"—in which terrorists attacked our office, and he defended us. I found it clever, and he was willing to work for free for a while, so there you go."

A little note of worry crept into Christine's voice: "Every

fan on the planet is going to realize the heart you have, and our life—everyone's going to be like 'Hi! I'm going to be your intern!'"

"Jeff is the one screening the fan mail?" I asked.

"No, Christine's the backstopper," Sean explained. "Don't you read everything?"

Christine answered obliquely, "Jeff's the softhearted one who reads it. He's the one who goes, 'Oh, this is a special case, we need to answer this one personally.' He's very"— a tactful pause—"sensitive."

Sean even met Jim, who occasionally works as his bodyguard, because Jim's twelve-year-old daughter asked Sean for his autograph. Jim, a six-foot, two-hundred-pound Baloo bear of a man, later explained to me, "A problem for us protectors is that we're fans, too. But we can't let that interfere with doing our duty of making sure nobody bothers them." He has been working on a movie script that he hopes Sean will help him sell.

That night, I asked if I could spend the day with Sean as he prepared for and entered a red-carpet event, and he suggested the Screen Actors Guild Awards. He said that Gibson would arrange for me to come with him, although Gibson, as it turned out, wasn't so wild about this idea.

When I spoke with her the following week, she said, "This is not simple. This is very complicated. This is much more complicated than you might think it is." I expressed my appreciation for the difficulty, then asked whether, since Sean had said he'd like me to come, she might be able to help by putting in a word with SAG. "I can't make that call for you," she said, and looked up and read to me the general telephone number for the Screen Actors Guild. I asked if she at least knew the name of the person who was handling the credentials, and she said, "No, I don't know anyone there. I don't know who handles this stuff."

About a dozen calls later I secured a credential, and the morning of the SAG Awards, Sean sent a shiny black limousine to take me to Disney's Imagineering campus, where I watched him record DVD commentary for *The Two Towers*. When he'd finished, the DVD's producer asked Sean to sign a picture for the operator who'd made his reservation at the Biltmore Hotel, where he would be staying that night. The operator had burst into tears when the producer told her the room was for Sean, whom she'd called "my favorite, favorite actor of all time in the whole wide world."

Then I tagged along with him to the Beverly Hills Hotel for a SAG Awards "pre-party" in honor of *The Hours* hosted by Sherry Lansing and Jonathan Dolgen, then co-chairs of Paramount Pictures. When we stepped out of the car, the air felt cool and green, and the bellmen greeted Sean by name. He asked how they were, and one said, "We promise not to call you Samwise Gamgee!" and waved us to the Polo Lounge, where the piano struck up "Nice 'n' Easy" as we advanced to the veranda, crowded with people like Daryl Hannah, David Hare, and Red Buttons, all eating from a table piled with fresh berries, salmon, and eggs in puff pastry with caviar.

The whole room looked when Sean entered, and older women kept walking up to him and saying, "We loved your mother." Michael Moore and his wife and producer Kathleen Glynn approached him and Michael said, "We love you. You're great."

"No," Sean said, "you're great." They swapped compliments for *Bowling for Columbine* and the *Lord of the Rings* movies, and Michael gave Sean his address so he could send him a signed poster for his kids.

Moments later, Linda Blair and Cuba Gooding Jr. each said, "You're great, Sean," and Sean said, "You're great," twice.

Moments after that, Sean said, "I love you," to Jennifer Beals, who blinked at Sean and said, "I love your work."

She looked exactly like a doe, and her poise gave me a hunch that her response was more than automatic—a hunch confirmed when I interviewed her the following year and we talked about the constant compliments that come when an actor scores a hit. "Fame is other people's perceptions of you," she said, choosing her words carefully. "Whenever anybody compliments you, it's their perception of you. It's not who you are. In those little quiet moments during the day or night, that's who you are. Other people's perceptions of you change constantly. They're like an ocean that's constantly in turmoil."

Sean met his wife, Christine, and changed into a tux at the Biltmore downtown, then we all piled in the limo for the short trip to the Shrine Auditorium.

With the windows rolled down, we passed a family in a beat-up Ford who recognized Sean and started waving madly and swerving. "Hi! Hi! Nice to see you!" Sean said, and Christine, all but inaudible under her smile, issued a solicitous, singsongy curse of concern: "*You're going to get in a wreck! And it's going to be all your fault!*"

We saw protesters near the Shrine holding signs—MOVIE IDOLS REPENT and GLORIFY GOD, NOT YOURSELVES—and then the car stopped and we jumped out into a wave of high-pitched screams and rumbling hollers, with "Rudy!" and "Sam!" the only clear words in the noise. Sean waved and beamed, and Gibson the publicist led us through metal detectors and on the red carpet, where *Access Hollywood* corralled Sean, and I stood back.

The week before, while I was arranging credentials, Gibson had given me instructions: "On the red carpet, I will tell you how close to Sean you can get, how far away you have to stand. If you get too close, I'll give you what they call my evil eye"—she giggled—"and it's nothing towards you, it's just what I do, to make sure everything goes the right way. Everyone knows about it. *They call it my evil eye!*" This really cracked her up. "You have to follow all of the instructions *exactly*. It's very complicated. It's not simple. And if you don't follow all of the instructions exactly, it will blow up in your *face*."

My face, so far, was in one piece, so while Sean talked to *Access Hollywood*, I focused on the packed bleachers, a wall of people about twenty feet high whose presence was uncanny. One minute it felt good having a wall of people alongside us, cheering for the guy that I was here with— and the next minute, I just wanted out of there, because their screams for each star seemed identical but for the name, which made their desire seem sometimes frighten- ingly, sometimes fatuously, indiscriminate.

Sean broke from the interviews, turned to wave at the crowd, and a borderline-pubescent girl in a tummy-show- ing tank top and almost obscenely low-rise jeans screamed, "*Come here please!*" and Sean hollered, "I'm sorry, I can't!" and turned to me to say, "I don't want to think about why she's dressed the way she's dressed," at the moment when a huge Samoan man in an orange shirt jumped to his feet and roared out, "*Rudy!*"

Sean roared right back, a friendly "*Hey!*" to which the big guy smiled, fell silent, as if charmed, and sat back down.

The crowd's rhythm was exactly as Sean had described it in the car a few minutes before: "With these fans, every fifteen seconds to a minute during the sweet spot of the arrivals, there will be a swell all of a sudden—*whoosh!* There will be a rush, and you can almost feel it, like somebody picks up the carpet and an emotional wave goes through everybody, all the journalists in the middle of their interviews, you can feel their energy wondering who it is while they're talking to you."

Sean was moving down the press line, and each reporter asked what he was wearing, and what his wife was wearing, and "How do you feel?" and Sean said, "I feel great!" Most of the reporters were women in cheap evening gowns, and several held clipboards with their magazine's title pasted on the back, so that the celebrities could keep track of who they were talking to. The reporters' eyes were weirdly wired to their tongues, so that in every pause in conversation, they would scan the carpet, making sure that no big fish swam by unseen.

Even so, no two eyes could take all this in. Behind Sean stars were colliding all over. Uma Thurman hugged Dennis Quaid, who was flying high with *Far from Heaven*: "Congratulations! You're so great!"

Dennis Quaid, with that sharp grin: "Oh, *you're* great!"

Uma—"Thank you!"—walking on, and then the same words, and the same response, from star to star to star.

This lovefest made the Polo Lounge look small-time, and when I tried to think if I had ever had a day like this, where so many human beings told me flat out, *You are great*, my mind went back to high school graduation. At the open house we had, even grouchy neighbors whom I hadn't really talked to since I was little came and hugged me, and after everyone had gone home I had a hundred Hallmark cards to open. Even though I knew that day would pass, that we were caught up in a ritual of exaggerated niceness, I remember feeling happy that, for a little while, the world seemed more abounding with good wishes than it usually seemed to be.

For Sean, and Dennis Quaid, and anyone who'd had a movie that hit big this year, every day right now had that same quality, blown up to billboard size. And yet, all this intrastellar adoration seemed, finally, almost as repetitive and indiscriminate as the crowd's bullish "Hey"'s and come-hither "Come here now"'s.

Near the end of the red carpet, Sean put his arm around my shoulders, gestured toward the fans, and smiling, asked, "Aren't you glad you're over here instead of over there?"

It almost seemed like he was gloating, which would have been out of character, but I said yes, to see what he was getting at.

"Do you know what the difference is?" he asked.

I shook my head.

"About two feet."

When Sean had disappeared into the Shrine, with Queen Latifah on his heels, Gibson said, "I need that now," and held her hand out for my press badge.

As she silently walked me to the exit, I tried making nice with a little humor: "Did I get the evil eye?"

"No, you did okay," she said. "I hope you got whatever you need."

Yes, I told her, I got to see what life was like on the red carpet. And even though she'd done her best to block my being there, I was flush with fellow feeling after such a thrilling day, so I thanked her for helping make it possible for me to come.

"Oh, please," she said. "It was nothing. All the SAG people and everyone who does the credentials—they're all really good friends of mine."

Across the street from where we had stepped onto the red carpet, I saw a group of fans who'd been screaming for Sean when we arrived, so I went over to say hi, and the tape of our conversation is a riot of praise and excitement that also contains the most coherent, if loopy, expressions of enthusiasm I'd heard all day:

"Isn't Sean the nicest guy?"

"Do you want to see his signature? I got it last year, let me show you!"

"Sean and I have a mutual friend."

"He is very intelligent and sweet. A very nice person. And so enthusiastic. He's such a Tolkien fan!"

They showed me Elvish jewelry they had made, and scrapbooks they were carrying around to pore over together while they stood in the sun waiting for arrivals. Everyone in the group—a few had already gone home, but the seven remaining would stay to watch the stars leave— said they were longtime Tolkien readers. They lived in the San Diego area but had not met until the films came out.

The movies, they explained, had inspired a network of Web sites that organized social events where they'd met and become friends.

One fan, a public-school teacher, said, "It's a beautiful symmetry that working on the movies made the actors fans of Tolkien, and I've never been a fan of actors before. I used to be offended by people who asked for autographs, but now here I am standing outside an awards show yelling '*Sean!*'" They all thought Sean was the bee's knees, but they weren't there so much because they thought he was intrinsically "great," as because "he loves Tolkien, and that makes it easy to love him, for loving what we love."

The next time I saw these fans was Oscar night, at a *Lord of the Rings* fan party at the Hollywood Athletic Club, where many of the trilogy's cast and crew showed up to mingle after the ceremony was over. That night I also met Kathleen Hanover, a freelance publicist from Ohio who couldn't quite believe her luck in being here. Before she'd left for California, she'd asked her coworkers, " 'Wouldn't it be awesome if I got to go to this party and talk with the stars?' And they were like, 'Sure, you keep thinking that, Kathleen.'" But she was determined.

She'd made herself a gorgeous Byzantine-style dress ("It's what I would wear to Aragorn's coronation if I were invited"), matched with slippers ordered from India and wire earrings that she had twisted into elaborate shapes in the front seat of her rental car in the parking lot of the Athletic Club. This costume, I later learned, gave only a glimpse of her creative abilities. She is an accomplished swing dancer and has written dozens of Burma Shave ads in honor of *The Lord of the Rings*:

Our profits soon
Would look so sweet
If hobbits chose
To shave their feet.
Burma Shave

I asked her to tell me about her favorite character in the films, and she said, "Sam. Absolutely." When I asked why, she said, "Sam is a regular person, a normal person. He'll never live in a palace or marry a queen. But he has a part to play in the grand drama of the world. He goes and he does that, but he'll come back to an everyday life in the end. That's what a hobbit is." With a gesture around the room full of fans, she said, "That's what we're like."

A couple of minutes after that, when Sean walked into the party, she was too shy to say hello, so I brought him over and told him there was someone I thought he should meet.

"Oh, my God, I love you so much," she told him. He hugged her, wrapped one arm around her waist, and introduced her to Christine. Kathleen pressed the button on her tape recorder and asked, "What was the most profound thing you learned about yourself making these movies?"

Sean gave her an intensely appreciative look that reminded me of the way he'd looked at me when we'd first met, when he'd told me that he thought we would be lifelong friends. He said, "That is the best question that anyone has ever asked me," and Kathleen was glowing like a torch.

Then after thinking for a minute, he said, "I learned that I do have an imagination, and I have just begun to scratch the surface of it."

When I called Kathleen a year later to reminisce about the night, she still cherished that moment of contact, and with wonder, she quoted Sean's compliment to her again. "To think that I asked Sean Astin the best question anyone has ever asked him just amazes me. If I could have written a script for that evening, I could not have ended it in a more magical way. I had my little tape recorder with me, and I listen to it again sometimes, so I know that it really happened."

Sean and I e-mailed a lot during that spring and summer. Late one night he wrote a long message about, among other things, the challenge of sorting his e-mail in-box. He wasn't sure where to put me: "I spent five minutes once all of your e-mails were in a file trying to stick your name under a heading . . . publicity, work, and some of the other tortured headings just didn't feel right . . . so I put you under the plain heading of friend."

I had always felt a little bit uncomfortable with Sean's calling me his friend. I had said, on several occasions, that while I could imagine our becoming friends, for now our relationship would be professional. But he kept coming back to that word. This time I gave in, because I really enjoyed his company, and also because I was flattered that this famous guy had chosen me to be part of his world. I responded that, as a journalist, getting to know the people I write about sometimes blurs the categories of personal and professional life, but that "I, like you, try to err on the side of generosity when I try to categorize people. So 'friend' works well by me."

That said, I decided to go out on a limb in this same e-mail and speak more personally to Sean than I had before. I told him that I'd just gone with my dad and sister to my mom's family farm in Kansas, where we'd scattered her ashes in a field. On that trip I'd had an odd moment of feeling connected with Sean:

> My sister and I went out to antique shops [and found] a set of "Addams Family" playing cards. I flipped through them, and lo and behold: there was Gomez. It was strange, seeing him—I used to watch reruns of that show every day after school—and now thinking of him not only as Gomez, but also as Sean's Dad.

His response:

> I got a real kick out of the Addams Family stuff story . . . I was moved picturing you with your Dad and sister scattering your Mom's ashes. I wrote a poem in college about [that] called "Cremation," I hope it's in my files somewhere. I have posted a couple bits of poetry online. It makes me feel good to think other people read it, the tidbits of feedback that my webmaster forwards to me really make me feel good.

Exchanges like this threw the ambiguities of my relationship with Sean into relief. When you tell a friend that you just got back from scattering your dead mom's ashes, you hope for a little more in the way of understanding than I-wrote-a-poem-called-"Cremation." Then again, if you're a reporter doing a job, you generally don't share your personal stuff with a movie star.

When I told a friend of this exchange, a man who has a lot of experience being friends with stars, he gave me a talking-to that went something like this: *That's how celebrity friendship works. Sean Astin is a talented guy. But there are twenty guys who could have played Rudy, twenty guys who could have played Sam. He goes to audition after audition where it turns out he's not good-looking enough, he's not hot enough, he's not bankable enough. Sometimes people say those things to his face. To endure that, to succeed the way he has, a star has got to have an ego that's so strong it crowds out lots of other things, like the capacity for empathy with almost any other person. And sooner or later, an ego like that will freeze out everyone in your life except the ones who are your fans.*

I got to know Sean pretty well, but not well enough to judge for certain whether my friend's description of celebrity friendship was completely on the mark in this case. I know that Sean was trying clumsily to reach out to me. After several exchanges like the e-mails you just read, I also came to think that it was more fun wanting to be part of Sean's world than trying to be.

Just before we had left the party at the Polo Lounge, Sean had pulled me aside and quietly said, "It's amazing to get to the point where you're not so amazed that you can get into a party like this that you can actually watch what's going on. And then see, all around you, who's doing what, all the exchanges and transactions in the room, start getting some idea of how it all works."

Having been brought up by famous parents, and having been a celebrity in his own right at least since *The Goonies* (when he was fourteen), Sean has been to so many parties and red carpet events that it was hard to believe he could feel like an outsider in such settings. But another story he told me suggested that his parents' fame may actually have sharpened his sense of exclusion from starworld—and that the Wall of Fame can extend even into a celebrity's own family.

Hanging out with his dad at a coffee shop, "I had been sharing with him different experiences. I was explaining in a way, like, 'Dad, you don't understand. When I get on an airplane, when I'm in a restaurant . . .' "—Sean laughed— "I would almost forget who I was talking to. He could probably understand exactly what I'm talking about."

John Astin, he said, "looked me in the eyes and said, 'You've really experienced your first taste of celebrity.' It was dawning on him at the moment he was saying it, in a way that was like, I had just been invited into a different room that I hadn't been into before. It was like, I've arrived now, to his standard of experience."

Then, Sean said, he understood, "I've got something in common with this man that I didn't realize. And it made it feel a little bit more safe. Being a second-generation celebrity person, I found it reassuring." (Sean had asked his dad to come along to this interview, but John had vehemently refused, for reasons that he either didn't tell Sean or Sean didn't want to tell me, except to make a *whoo-boy* face and say, "He really didn't like that idea at all.")

For everyone, the relief of finally relating to parents as peers is hard-won. I wondered whether, for Sean, reaching that point was complicated by the presence of a Wall of Fame in his own family—a separation that could finally dissolve only with the shared experience of celebrity. Maybe you have to get over a hurdle of fame to feel at home with your dad, I asked, because you always knew him not only as your dad, but as a star?

"May be," he said, nodding his head up and down. "May be. May be." Then he laughed again, a slightly uncomfortable guffaw that he sometimes made when conversation strayed into territory he hadn't thought about before. "I bet if my dad heard you say that, he would rage against it, like, 'No way, that isn't it at all.' But I'd be, like, 'No, Dad, that is part of it.' I'm sure of it."

Even Sean's daughter, Alexandra, had figured out, by the time she was seven, that her dad's fame made him essentially different from her. After describing the experience of finally becoming a peer in celebrity with his dad, Sean said:

"I like people-surfing—I know what Marilyn Monroe meant when she said that she turned on Marilyn as opposed to being Norma Jean. I know what that feels like. There's a thing of confidence or pride or dignity or extrovertedness that, if I want, I can switch it on, and it's amazing what happens.

"It's a little unsettling because people resent it, too. People who are close to you, who see that by clicking into that mode you can get a free upgrade on a flight, you can get a seat at a restaurant.

"Allie loves to mock me that I can get whatever I want by just asking for it: 'You're an actor, you're Sean Astin, you can just get whatever you want.'

"I say, 'I don't get whatever I want.'

" 'Yes, you do. You get shoes, you get this, you get that.' She goes through this catalog of things that I get that I don't pay for."

His daughter's teasing shouldn't be confused with jealousy. Quite the opposite: as Sean told it, Allie didn't want any part of her dad's fame. (She did play a small part as an

Elvish princess in *The Fellowship of the Ring* when she was four, but Sean said that was mostly because she wanted to wear the pretty dress and pretend to be an elf.) When the whole family visited an Indiana fairground on the Fourth of July, "there were some guys playing football, and I'm like, 'Hey! Throw me the ball!' But you make one gesture like that, you make eye contact, and—Alexandra has a wonderful phrase for what happens. She calls it a people storm. She always notes when a people storm is about to happen. She will either cling on me very tightly, or else Christine."

When Sean told Alexandra he was going to be photographed for an ad campaign, and that the sponsor had offered her the option of being in the ad with him, "she was like, 'Will people ask me for my autograph?'

"I said, 'A lot of people would see it, so they would probably recognize you if you did it.'

"She said, 'No, I don't want to be in the middle of a people storm. I don't want that.'"

I couldn't get Alexandra to expound on this for me. (She doesn't like reporters, although when Sean told her that I was "a nice reporter," she grabbed a box of crayons and started showing me her favorite colors.) Allie's aversion to people storms makes sense, though, even without further elaboration.

Imagine you're a seven-year-old girl, moving daily back and forth between two worlds: a comfortable house with a loving family, where you're the apple of your daddy's eye—and the world outside your house, where wild-acting strangers might at any moment try to push their way between you. What could be more frightening than a people storm?

A people storm makes Daddy into something called Sean Astin. Like an ocean that is constantly in turmoil, it beats on him with waves of words: *We loved your mother, Sam!* and *Rudy! Come here please!* and *You are great.* People storms are all the free shirts, leather duffel bags, and e-mails, the screams and glances, the poems and the tape recordings, every effort that fans make to reach the star we think we could hang out with, every wish we have to be part of his world of fame. We make people storms to hide the cool, small truth that Allie knows: a people storm is the opposite of home.

Every so often, there comes along a movie or a TV show that by showing characters who remind you of yourself, has the power to make you feel more at home in the world. When it debuted in 1998, *Will & Grace* had that power for me. The year before, when I had just started dating men, I'd experienced *Ellen*'s coming out as an almost sanctifying moment. It was kind of like when, as a teenager, I'd seen St. Louis in a movie for the first time. A blink-and-miss-it scene in *Planes, Trains, & Automobiles*, where that city is just a troublesome obstruction in Steve Martin's tortured journey home. But still. St. Louis was the closest major city to my middle-of-nowhere town. It was a place I had a claim on. And it was in a movie!

Walker Percy, in *The Moviegoer* (1961), called this feeling "certification":

> Nowadays when a person lives somewhere, in a neighbor-
> hood, the place is not certified for him. More than likely he
> will live there sadly and the emptiness which is inside him
> will expand until it evacuates the entire neighborhood. But

if he sees a movie which shows him his very neighborhood, it becomes possible for him to live, for a time at least, as a person who is Somewhere and not Anywhere.

Or Nowhere, as the case may be. Having grown up in a culture where gay people were practically invisible, except for the occasional camp figure or AIDS patient (or, more often, "victim"), I felt that same relief when *Ellen* drew the spotlight to my neighborhood. Soon, though, the show's (or network's) discomfort with its character's (and star's) disclosure led to the series being canceled, which raised a discouraging possibility. Maybe my neighborhood belonged in blackout, after all.

Then along came *Will & Grace*, showing stories about gay men for everyone to see. And people watched it. So what if Jack was silly? So what if Will was sexless? I could watch them from my sofa and think, *These guys are gay like me—and on TV. And the straight world loves them, too.* It was a comfort just to have them in the ether, and it strengthened the belief that my life didn't need to be a secret. There was some dignity in that.

For a few lean years, I didn't have cable (and got bad reception with the rabbit ears), so I didn't see much of *Will & Grace* after that first heady season. When I moved to L.A., I started watching it again, and I didn't like it much. The show's scripts had devolved into a weekly barrage of insult and self-congratulation, lumped into some semblance of plot by the presence of an A-list celebrity guest star. Plus, Will Truman, despite having every qualification for being the perfect catch, still didn't have a boyfriend. *Will & Grace* had become *The Love Boat*, without the love.

I looked back to some older episodes in syndication. To my surprise, I found most only marginally better. I wondered why I'd been so taken with these selfish characters, and I realized, there had been few other options. *Will &
Grace* came along at a time when I was grateful for any models I could find for helping me figure out how to be myself. Then I'd stopped watching because I couldn't afford cable—but one of the reasons I couldn't afford cable was that I was spending the money on going out with friends. When I started getting a life, I didn't need the escape or guidance of this TV show anymore. And yet, *Will & Grace* had been a crucial source of comfort that bred the confidence I'd needed to get the life that took away my need for *Will & Grace*. Still, my reassessment of the show revealed more than my own evolution.

The show's celebrity blur and its avoidance of Will's love life had eroded its integrity. The result was a downward spiral that looked a lot like what can happen in a gay man's life if he decides that coming out consists merely of making that announcement to the world. Men who make that mistake can end up with lives that resemble what this show was increasingly becoming—a mess of caustic relationships, meaningless story lines, and the endless pursuit of distant, idealized objects of desire.

After Matt Damon, Elton John, Minnie Driver, Glenn Close, Michael Douglas, Demi Moore, Kevin Bacon, Gene Wilder, and Cher had all appeared on the show, NBC announced another guest star: in her prime-time network-series debut, Madonna would be coming to *Will & Grace*. This show's creators and cast were virtually unknown when they'd debuted five years before. Now they were among the most successful and famous people in television, and their studio had become a world that A-list celebrities were clamoring to get into. Publicity for the show sometimes described its celebrity guests as "fans" of *Will & Grace* and used the same word to describe cast members' feelings for the guests. Madonna's visit to the world of *Will & Grace* promised to test the hype of star-on-star fandom.

And the taping of her appearance on the show was almost certain to set off a people storm in the bleachers, since *Will & Grace* is one of the few sitcoms whose live audience consists primarily of true fans. "Audience procurement services," a term that deftly blends efficiency and sleaze, are hired by networks to recruit groups to fill the seats at most shows. *Will & Grace* uses a company called Audiences Unlimited, one of whose employees admitted to me that they have to beg, borrow, and steal to get bodies in the studios for most sitcoms. Tickets for *Will & Grace*, however, are just about the easiest sell they have. "Gay people who have been watching this show forever kind of think the show is about them," she said, "and they go kind of nuts to see it live."

As often happens when mortals meet their idols, many involved with *Will & Grace* found meeting Madonna a bit of a letdown. "She shows up and she does this thing where she pretends like she doesn't remember anybody's name, and I guess it makes her feel good about herself," said Max Mutchnick, one of the show's creators and executive producers. "That might be impressive for some development executive who's happy to be in the room with her. But it doesn't fly here."

According to some who were present at rehearsals, Eric

McCormack was openly offended that Madonna arrived in what seemed to be total ignorance of his name. When I asked about it, he offered a heavily qualified account of the fracas: "She did ask me my name a couple of times, and I said, 'It's easy, just check the opening credits of the other one hundred and twenty of these that we've done.' She sort of laughed, but I was sort of only half-kidding. But by shoot night, I had to admit that she had been very professional all week. And then she sort of made up for it at the end of the week, when she sent me the most expensive thing of roses I've ever seen, and a card from her saying, 'Eric, Thank you so much. I'm gonna have your name tattooed on my arm, if Guy [Ritchie, her husband] will let me.'" Then he looked at me and said, "You have to write that I was laughing as I said this."

Of everyone who discussed the singer's forgetfulness, Megan Mullally was the least perturbed: "I mean, it's Madonna." She laughed. "No other rules apply." Sean Hayes was the most pragmatic: "I love Madonna, but how I feel about Madonna is unimportant. We are in business to get ratings. People like to watch stars like Madonna. We have stars, we get ratings."

And Eric McCormack, once he'd gotten the story of that snub off his chest, opened up the political possibilities of Sean's pragmatic comment: "I think as soon as there is any indication that there's no celebrities this week, but Will's going to be on a date, [viewers] get scared off. A tree falls in the forest and nobody hears it, then what's the point? People are going to watch the Madonna episode that have never watched the show before. It'll probably be our biggest episode. If that's the case, damn! Let's have that number of people show up to watch me hold George

Clooney's hand or whoever's up for doing it. It would be a very good use of stunt casting." That was an interesting thought: maybe you have to kiss a lot of Madonnas before you get to hold somebody's hand.

Sitcom tapings are tedious (six hours is a short one), but for Madonna's appearance on the set of *Will & Grace*, NBC received about 600 requests for the studio's 206 seats, and 75 percent of the final audience were VIPs. This, according to the show's publicist, Jamie, a quick-witted guy who always shared his cigarettes with me. (This was when I thought that if I bummed them, I wasn't a real smoker.)

I saw a lot of people I knew. The screenwriter who had skipped my dinner party to have drinks with Uma (and was once the subject of a cover story in *Only Child* magazine) waved to me from the front row of the audience. One of the Paramount publicists I'd met while reporting on Mary Hart was there, and when I asked why he'd come, the man's partner interrupted, "He's had a poster of Madonna in his office for like twenty years!" The publicist winced, but managed a wan smile. "Once I met her at a little dinner party thrown by some friends," he said, prideful and mortified. "I was retarded. I couldn't say anything. I don't have to meet her tonight. I just want to be close to the action."

When Madonna appeared on set to shoot her first scene, Megan Mullally introduced her to the audience as "a woman who needs no introduction: Madonna." The whole audience jumped to its feet. Screams. Cheers. Then Roger Lundblade, the audience warm-up guy, calmed them down so shooting could continue. (Every sitcom has one of these: they tell jokes and give out free candy bars to help stave off hypoglycemia. Audience warm-up guys are usually failed comedians, and they always have steady incomes.)

After the first few takes (even the flubbed ones), the audience popped up again to give Madonna a standing ovation, and a few fans kept hollering, "I love you!"

Eventually the group chilled out enough that Roger Lundblade started answering questions from the audience. A young Hispanic man named Javier asked, about Madonna, "Can I meet her?"

"Just your friendly neighborhood stalker!" Roger answered. "Ha ha ha ha . . ."

When I scribbled down the line, Jamie said, "I'm nervous. What are you writing in that notebook?"

"Mrs. Jamie Publicist," I told him. "Mrs. James E. Publicist."

Jamie went over to talk to a magazine editor, who, when I joined them a few minutes later, greeted me with catty playfulness: "Jamie was just saying how much he hates you."

Jamie said, "It's true."

Jamie's boss mendingly interjected, "And after that he was saying sweet things about you."

Jamie glared at her and said, "It's *all* about the love. *Hey!* Did you see the boy in the Hawaiian shirt who kissed Debra's hand and started crying?"

"Crocodile tears," said the editor, and Jamie said, "Totally. I was like, 'Sister! Pull it together! Pop a Valium!'" They both laughed hard.

Somehow I'd missed this, but they pointed out the "boy" in question, and I kept an eye on him. At the end of the next take, he sprang up in his seat and waved to Debra, who stepped forward and waved back. His jaw dropped and he put his hand to his heart, like a maiden in a silent movie.

Aghast, Jamie rushed to Debra and said, "My *God*, can you believe that guy?"

For a second, she looked tempted to join in Jamie's scoffing, the way you often do when friends start making fun of an awkward stranger on the street. Then she pulled back and changed the subject.

Going up into the audience, I found the Hawaiian shirt and introduced myself to Chad Evans, a twenty-year-old Starbucks barista from Boston with the watery dark eyes of a night owl. When I asked him how it felt to be there, it was as if I'd pulled his thumb out of a dike. "It is the best day of my life," he began, and said he watches *Will & Grace* every night in syndication at eleven-thirty, and that he hasn't missed a first-run episode since the show came on the air. The cast of the show, he said, "are all my favorite stars," for reasons that sounded familiar to me. "They give you hope that you don't have to hide. You don't have to be invisible."

He said that he could not believe that Debra had reached out to him. "It just proves she's real," he explained. "She's looking out. She knows there's somebody out there and she's trying to make them happy. She's not just a star in big sunglasses. Some people, if they're a celebrity and they see someone freaking out like me, might pull away, but she called me down, and she just seemed like a completely real person."

He then turned around, raised up his shirt, and showed

me a tattoo: the logo of Madonna's Drowned World tour, which he'd seen in New York a couple of years before. "She is my other favorite star," he said. "I just love her so much. Because of her I have faith in myself, and I persevere. And she is five or ten feet away from me! It's like I'm dreaming. I feel lucky to be alive in the same time she is. She's been the only constant when times were down or hard. She's not just an entertainer. She's like a spiritual figure. Anybody that ever gives her shit, it's because they're jealous that they can't be like she is themselves."

He began to cry. "I'm sorry that I look like this. It's just, all of this is a double whammy. It's not even like being starstruck. It's a whole separate entity."

When I asked what that meant, more tears flowed. "I don't know. I don't know . . ."

He said that he'd given a letter to Debra to give to Madonna—four handwritten pages ("I told her, 'I don't want anything from you . . . I've written and rewritten this . . .'")—along with a $10 Starbucks gift card, and suggestion: "I know you like soy lattes, but I'd like you to try the soy hazelnut chai." He said he didn't expect her to answer, but several times he told me that he just hoped she'd try the chai.

After that I went back down onto the set and introduced myself to Debra Messing, telling her I'd just finished talking with her paramour. Her eyes lit up: "Tell me what he said!"

Cautiously attentive, she listened and nodded, and when I finished reading, she said, "It sounds like he doesn't really understand that this is special to me, too. I wanted him to know it was real. Because his reaction was so explosive and so out of the realm of what I would consider reasonable. So I wanted to touch him and show him, 'Hey, I am real. I'm a person. And this is what I do for work.' And I appreciate him. In a different way than he appreciates me, but in a way that's also powerful. That this is not a one-sided relationship."

After the taping was finished, a Warner Bros. Records employee was herding her radio-contest winners to one corner of the set where they'd been told they would meet Madonna and have their picture taken with her. There looked to be about thirty of them, and their pictures with the singer were taken in groups of about ten. When it was Chad's turn to have his picture taken, he was working hard to control his breathing, and pressing the palm of his right hand against his open mouth.

Madonna gave him a frightened look, and when he said hello, she would not speak to him. I watched her through-out what the Warner Bros. woman had told me would be a "meet and greet" with the fans, but the only word Ma-donna spoke, as far as I could tell, was to a stout, short woman in Chad's photo group who sidled up to her and said, "This is the second time I've won this contest!" Looking straight into the camera, Madonna rolled her eyes and said, "Grea-eat," riding the vowel for an extra syllable, like a snobby girl in grade school.

Jamie walked me to the door of the soundstage. Putting on a grand voice, he said, "The magic of the dream factory. Oh, baby, *the Magic. Of. The Dreams!*"

The crew, closing down the set after the shoot, was still talking about Chad, joking that he might be a stalker. "We should track that guy for six months," one said.

Jamie flipped his box of Marlboros toward me, but I

said I was fine, and he lit up as we walked out into the dark.

The next day I drove to the Sheraton in Universal City and picked up Chad and his friend Amanda Pierce, a twenty-four-year-old veterinary technician from Boston. (Amanda had won the Warner Bros. contest and had brought Chad along as her guest.) As we drove around Hollywood, they told me, in thick Boston accents, how they'd first met six years earlier when Amanda was smoking pot in Harvard Square and trying to study for an exam.

"This guy rolls up to me and says, 'Hi, I'm Chad!' and starts writing the lyrics to 'Ray of Light' in my notebook," Amanda remembered. She didn't get much studying done, but she found a new best friend.

Chad, at the time, was a student at Arlington Catholic High School with big dreams of stardom. He had once appeared in an elementary school cabaret revue, performed in summer camp talent shows (one year, he sang "Like a Prayer"), and he had a three-line part in a high school production of *Damn Yankees*. (He had "creative differences" with the director—specifically, "she was a bitch"—and decided drama club was not for him.)

After high school, Chad had started working at Starbucks and saving his money to move to Hollywood. He didn't seek out any more theatrical experience because "Boston theater is too depressing." In the meantime he was living with his parents. His father is a lawyer, his mother "works for Mass. General Hospital in the infectious-disease unit doing exactly what I can't tell you, because I don't know. It's kind of sad." His parents, he said, are somewhat skeptical of his ambition: "All the time I tell my mother, 'I'm going to be a star, I'm going to be a star,' and she's like, 'Okay.' But I always told her, 'I'm going to meet Madonna one day,' and now I did. I don't want to get stuck in Boston. I don't want to go to school there. I just want to jump into acting. For me, going to school, I don't believe it's necessary to succeed. I could do what I saw last night with the snap of a finger. I was watching last night, and I kept thinking, 'I could do this.' It's just not that hard to become someone else, to take on a new personality."

Unlike his parents, Amanda has always supported Chad's ambitions. "I think he would be a great actor," she said. "He can make himself whatever he needs to be. We go places and he throws up a fake British accent, and people believe him, like when we were in Saks the other day."

At this point we were driving down Highland toward Hollywood Boulevard, and I pointed out the Hollywood Heritage Museum, in the small yellow barn that was the first film soundstage in Los Angeles. "Cecil B. DeMille and D. W. Griffith shot there," I said, and Chad said, "That's nice."

I asked Chad what he planned to do when he got to Hollywood, how he imagined he would go about becoming a star. He said, "I would definitely have my head shots taken. It's all about networking. Schmoozing and networking and auditioning. Charming people. Charm, charm, charm. But I don't want anything handed to me. I want to work for it so people won't resent me later and be like, 'This guy's just a pretty face.' That wouldn't be fulfilling to me at all."

He also talked about how exciting the previous night's taping had been. "I don't want to say I'm not starstruck," he began. "I know that stars are people. They're not just made up. But when it's Debra and Madonna—they're different because, I don't know. They can be completely happy."

How is that?

"You know, I don't know. I don't know. I'm just completely amazed. Like, seeing how small they were yesterday."

Amanda interrupted, "I was amazed at how small they were."

Chad, to keep one step ahead of Amanda, explained, "Because you look so huge in everything that you do in pictures. And I guess it's because they both have big mouths, it makes them look a lot taller than they are."

He turned back to me. "It's just amazing to finally, like, see them. I know that Debra Messing and Grace are two different people. But last night it was proven to me, that they are separate. And, I don't know. I'm tongue-tied."

Chad and Amanda wanted to see Madonna's star on Hollywood Boulevard and "to find a store where we can get Madonna memorabilia," so I took them to the Hollywood and Highland complex, where the Kodak Theatre was being readied for that weekend's Academy Awards.

I pointed out the red carpet on the staircase leading to the Kodak, and Chad said, "My first time on the red carpet. Joan Rivers will stand right over here somewhere." A security guard asked us to walk on the sidewalk instead of the carpet, and Chad was miffed: "Like we're not cool enough."

Then, looping back to topic A: "As far back as I can remember, I've always wanted to be an international icon.

And I have to believe it will happen, because I don't believe that life is that cruel."

Chad's ambition was spiking off the charts, and I kept probing for a sign that his grand design had room for alternatives. "Do you have a contingency plan in case becoming an international icon doesn't work out?" I asked.

He said, "There's just no other way. I don't see happiness coming to me in any other form."

"Why would it make you happy to be a star?"

Quick answer: "Because I could get my point across."

"What's your point?"

Quicker answer: "It's totally different things. I'm very strongly opinionated about things. Just anything at all. I always have something to say about everything. I want to be able to express that and be provocative and inspiring and, you know, be controversial and, you know, have my name on people's lips. I don't want to say that I just want the attention. But I definitely want the attention. It's in my nature. I can never explain why that has to be for me. But this is just the lifestyle that I feel that is right for me. It feels like destiny."

We walked up the street to Grauman's Chinese so they could see the hand- and footprints in the pavement. "Denzel Washington!" Chad said. "Mm-hmm. Big feet. You know?"

Amanda started giggling. "John Travolta! We just walked by John Travolta's footprints and didn't even stop!"

Chad: "Bette Davis! Bette Davis! I have to take a picture for my mom." Then, regaining his composure: "I look forward to being able to make somebody feel the way that I feel about the stars I love."

As impressed as he was with his visit to Hollywood, Chad was a little surprised by how "unritzy" the neighborhood was. "This place is not what I expected. It's more real. It's more attainable." The run-down face of Hollywood only added to his sense that "just to visit here a couple of days makes me even surer I can do this, surer that I'm going to be a star."

We were riding an escalator down to the underground lot where my car was parked. Mounted above the escalator are TV monitors that play advertisements in an endless loop. As Chad made that last remark, I glanced up to see an ad—maybe for a stunt show at a studio, maybe for some death-defying reality TV show—that showed a man on fire, falling through the air toward a pool of water.

Not too long after this, Debra Messing told me a story about her salad days as a drama student in London, when she decided to go see one of her idols, Dustin Hoffman, in *The Merchant of Venice*:

"I got nosebleed tickets because I had absolutely no money. I was trying to concoct some way of getting to meet him, and so I wrote my first and only fan letter. I enclosed a picture of myself, and I basically told him what he meant to me, and that I would love to meet him, I would be in the audience that night.

"But that wasn't enough for me. I got a little courageous that day, talking about this to my acting teacher, who encouraged me to go to the stage door. So I went to the stage door that afternoon with the letter, and the stage manager blocked me, and so in order to get the letter to him, I lied, and I said, 'Hello, my father directed Dustin in *Kramer v. Kramer*,' and the stagehand said, 'Oh my God, I know your father. I'm a huge fan.' 'No,' I said, changing my story, 'I said *Marathon Man*. My father directed Dustin in *Marathon Man*, and he insisted that I come by and drop off this letter for him. I'm going to be in the house tonight. Can you make sure he gets this letter?' So the stagehand said, 'Well, of course, of course we'll get him the letter,' and I said thank you. I acted as if I was theatrical royalty of some kind, because I knew that way the letter would get to him.

"And then that night, after the show, it was just hordes and hordes of people waiting for Dustin Hoffman, and the door would open, and someone from the show would come out, and then it would slowly close, and finally I realized that there was no way that he would come out that door with all those people there.

"So when the door flung open with one of the extras, one of the spear carriers, I tore through the crowd and snuck in as the door was closing, and the stagehand was a different person from that morning. He goes, 'Can I help you?' And I said, 'Oh, I'm here to see Dustin.' And I started to shake, but I told the same story: My father directed him in *Marathon Man*. I just thought I'd come by and say hi, just pop in and see him.

"He looked at me strangely, and he said, 'Stay here,' and I waited like eight minutes, and I was sweating, and all of a sudden the director of the play came down, and he said, 'May I help you?' And I said, 'I'm here to see Dustin.' He said, 'Come with me,' and I was like, oh my God, and we just started walking through this maze of a hall to the bowels of the theater by the dressing rooms, and he pointed up the stairs and said, 'That's where his dressing room is. He'll be down in a second.'

"We just stood there, and we're waiting and waiting, and the director was like, hm, maybe he went down the other way, and I started to panic, like, wait a minute, we missed him? And he said, 'Come on, let's go back around the other way,' and we started running down the hallway, and the door swung open, and there he was.

"Standing by the stage door. And I could not speak. And I remember just breaking down into sobs and handing him my program. And he was very nice. And I handed him a pen, and because the program was waxy, *it wasn't taking the pen*. And I started having a complete emotional breakdown. Because there he was. With the pen in hand. And it wasn't taking. And I was like, *do I need another pen?*

"He said, 'Hold on, I'll get one,' and he signed it. And I literally thought I was going to combust from the level of emotional intensity that I was feeling so I don't even remember saying good-bye. I don't recall saying thank-you. I just remember grabbing the autograph and running out the door and catching up with my friends and literally falling into pieces, just breaking down into sobs, and I couldn't speak for the rest of the night, and ten years later, I was at the People's Choice Awards, no, the American Comedy Awards, my first time presenting, and he was at the table next to me, and I went up to him and I just started shaking all over again. I just said, 'Excuse me, Mr. Hoffman, I met you ten years ago,' and before I knew it, I was hyperventilating and I was shaking, and Eric McCormack, who was with me, was laughing because he couldn't believe what a complete ridiculous mess I was. But Dustin Hoffman was lovely, and he was like, 'Well, I met you?' I said, 'I met you, I snuck in, and I was just an idiot . . .'

"But once I had met him, I felt like I had sort of fulfilled

215

something that was necessary in my life in order to continue on striving to be an actor, and now I can be thrilled
when I'm in the same room as him, but I don't ruin his tux
with tears anymore.

"Being a young actress in Rhode Island it was so difficult
to enter the life of being an actor. Everyone around you
encourages you not to because it's so uncertain. Everyone
who loves you is frightened that you're going to be hurt
and starving your entire life. So meeting Dustin Hoffman
was important as part of just plugging away and continuing to tell yourself that there's honor in the attempt.

"For me, watching Dustin Hoffman's movies as a teenager, doing drama club and planning my life to become an
educated actor, going to London, getting a master's de-
gree—anytime that I would question whether or not I
should consider going to law school instead, it was his
work that almost lit up my soul. It affected me and gave me
a feeling of purpose, for better or for worse, and allowed
me to continue to want to learn and to strive to be a part of
that world. And so to finally meet him, to be able to
articulate that to him—of course I'm sure I'm not the first
person to articulate it, but to the person who was so struck
and inspired by him, articulating it is sort of cathartic.
Being able to meet the source of your continuing forward
movement.

"Meeting him was something that felt like a sign. Like,
'Oh, yeah, you know what? I *should* be doing this.' The
fact that I've crossed paths with this person and had the
ability and the opportunity to express my gratitude to him
for what he has brought to the world and to me personally—it just felt like, okay, that's a sign that I really was
always supposed to be doing this."

I interrupted to ask if that gave her empathy for people like Chad, and she said:

"Yes. I felt like I understood him more than I understood me in that moment, if that makes sense.

"Because I had that kind of relationship with Dustin Hoffman, and I met him, and I could not control my emotions in his presence, and I feel no concern or shame about that. It was what it was, and it had to be that way—because of all the history, my own private history that I had with Dustin Hoffman that he knew nothing about.

"I recognized that in Chad. For some reason I'm blessed to be one of those people for him. I don't understand why, and I don't understand how I could be in any way an equivalent for him to Dustin Hoffman for me, because I don't see myself in the same category in terms of my innate gift. But that's not for me to say. Those relationships are incredibly personal and intimate. You can't control the development of those relationships. For someone it's Justin Timberlake. And for someone else, it's Al Pacino. For Chad, it was me and Madonna. Which I can't even believe I'm saying in one sentence. Of all things in my lifetime, the last thing I would ever believe is that I would be named in the same sentence with Madonna for anybody."

This was one of the smartest and most generous analyses of what happens when a fan gets close to fame that I have ever heard from a celebrity: "I felt like I understood him more than I understood me in that moment." When Chad met Debra, as when Debra met Dustin, it seemed like a sign that they might make it into the world they longed to enter. I am skeptical of that sign's usefulness for Chad, now that I know a little of his extravagant ambitions and his apparent ignorance of or disinterest in doing the work it would take to realize them. His naïveté and, it seems, laziness are so extreme they almost beg to be crushed.

One way to do that would be to argue this: Debra's fandom was different—higher and purer—because she respected Dustin's talent at least as much as his celebrity. For Debra, fandom had a purpose: to meet a man whose presence encouraged the work of shaping her own acting gift. For Chad, fandom only drives dead-end delusion: stardom is his destiny.

But that would not be fair. For one thing, I'd be comparing the excitement-in-the-moment of an aspiring barista with the distant memory of a major TV star. For another, Chad is twenty; and at that age, most of us have huge ambitions that have yet to find a proper form. Third, it's possible that Chad actually has talent—though if he did, and if he cared about it, he might be giving it some exercise. In any case, he hasn't learned, as Debra Messing has, what's appropriate to say out loud, and what he's best off keeping quiet. (When reporters ask actors what they would have done if they hadn't gotten that big break, the actors almost always say, "This was the only thing that I could do"—often true, and often code for a narcissistic faith in self at least as extreme as Chad's.)

Even the most skewed parts of his fantasy of fame—such as, if *Chad Evans* are not someday household words, it will mean the world is unimaginably cruel—not only state his specific dream of fame, but also claim, more basically, that he's worth looking at and listening to. He's not just the guy who makes your latte. He is *someone*.

In that way, this fan's dreams—even if they're shiftless—are anything but purposeless. Their purpose isn't yet as clear as that of Debra Messing's early dreams, except in one respect. The kind of fandom I have been describing—the fandom that aspires to claim a place, even for a moment, in the Technicolor world—longs for and can lead to an encounter where the fan makes himself known to a celebrity and is recognized, which makes him feel momentarily secure.

That security is fleeting. Fans know that stars forget them, and it stings to know that they become just faceless members of the crowd. When I told Chad that I talked with Debra about their meeting, he could not at first believe it: "Really? You talked about *me*?" Then he was worried: "What did she say? Did she think that I was crazy?" Shame and fear were already attacking the joy of his memory: yet more proof that a people storm is the opposite of home.

Even so, Chad still had one solid thing that would stay: "I can always say, 'I had a conversation with Debra Messing.'" The comfort of that memory will probably last, because of the way Debra treated him. As she said, "I wanted to touch him and show him, 'Hey, I am real.'" When a fan meets his favorite star, there is almost always a moment of disorienting, existential panic, and celebrities learn to calm fans down with a gesture to reassure them that we're all just piles of flesh. Or sometimes they use a phrase—like "That is the best question anyone has ever asked me" or "Send a letter to my office" or "I look forward to seeing you again"—to remind you that this encounter has not destroyed the space-time continuum, that both star and fan existed before this moment and will continue to exist when the moment's passed.

Sean Hayes told me, "I hug people when they come up to me because I want them to realize that I'm no more special than they are. It relaxes them, which relaxes me, and then we can connect. Nobody's better than anybody else, as much as they're perceived as that. We all have something to offer the world."

Such gestures are both generous and arrogant ways of relating to fans. Generous, because Sean Hayes thinks he means it when he says that he's no better than the people who look up to him. Arrogant, because presuming that fans need reassurance of their worth is to presume superiority to them. And yet, what else could he do? It's a catch-22. I think Sean's gesture of welcome to his world may be the best possible flawed response that he could make.

My most vivid experience of this kind of calming gesture came when I was about the age of Chad Evans when he met Debra Messing, which was about the age of Debra Messing when she met Dustin Hoffman. I was studying at Oxford for a year, and one day I took the bus to London to see a preview of *Six Degrees of Separation*, written by John Guare and starring Stockard Channing. The play is a Jack-and-the-beanstalk tale in which a poor young man who calls himself Paul cons his way into a Fifth Avenue apartment by pretending he's the son of Sidney Poitier. He charms and flatters Flan and Ouisa, the jaded, rich couple who live there, and then they learn that he's a fraud.

Nevertheless, Paul's desire to be a part of their world reawakens Ouisa's appreciation for the value of her own life, and of everyone's. Amazed at her own affection for

Paul, even after she finds out she's been conned, Ouisa marvels at "how every person is a new door, opening up into other worlds."

Much later I read an essay by Czeslaw Milosz that defined "the essence of theater" as "most likely, the human possibility of *being someone else*, which, if you think about it, means that every man is the home of many personalities that dwell within him potentially, that are never realized, because only one of them appears on the outside and proffers the mask that is accepted by others." *Six Degrees of Separation* is a play about precisely that possibility. In pretending to be someone other than himself, Paul opens Ouisa to the possibility of becoming a different kind of person, and more truly herself. Watching those transformations onstage strengthened my own faith in that possibility, too.

I loved the play so much that I convinced a friend to go back and see it with me a second time on opening night. When the curtain fell, I leaped to my feet and applauded till my hands stung. I roared, "*Bravo!*" It had not occurred to me that the whole theater would not be simultaneously exploding. It was not. My friend told me to sit down, but I didn't listen.

My brain flooded with endorphins, I sprinted up the street to find flowers for Stockard Channing, ducked into a convenience store, and slapped down money for some wilted daisies wrapped in clear cellophane, and I could not quite scrape off the price tag.

Back at the theater, I knocked on the stage door and asked the guard to please take these to Miss Channing. He said, "Just a minute," then closed the door. I waited and waited and finally he came back and said, "I'm sorry, I can't take those back for you," and panicking, I said, "Why not?"

"Because I think that you should take them back yourself."

He led me through the bowels of the theater and up to the stalls bar, where Stockard Channing and John Guare were sitting. "Thank you so much for your performance," I said, handing her the flowers and expecting her to dismiss me.

She said, "Won't you please sit down?"

They asked me what I studied and where I had grown up, and they listened to my gushing about how much I loved the play. I told them that I wanted to be a writer, and that I hoped I would someday write something that meant as much to someone as this play meant to me. My breath was short. I said "gosh" a lot. In a few minutes, I grew embarrassed of myself and said that it was time for me to go, and so I thanked them for talking to me, and John Guare said, "I look forward to seeing you again."

On the bus ride home to Oxford, I asked my friend, "Could you believe that? *He said he looked forward to seeing me again.*"

She explained that that was just good manners and that I should just calm down. She reproached me: "Those people live in a different world."

"I know," I said, humiliated by my own enthusiasm. I told her I was tired, closed my eyes, leaned my head against the cold glass window of the bus, and wrestled in myself, whether to accept my friend's reproach. I knew that she was probably right. I would be deluding myself if I thought a famous playwright would remember me a month from then, and I did not want to delude myself. And yet if she was right, then my dreams of living in the world of people like Stockard Channing and John Guare were all for nothing, and I might as well give them up. For a very young man with very big dreams, that could mean despair.

So on that bus ride, I decided I would take a middle way: I would neither believe nor disbelieve that I would ever see John Guare again. Instead, I'd hope that maybe, whether he had meant the words he had said or not, they had meaning. That it was not beyond the realm of possibility that a fan could mean something to a star. That a famous person like John Guare could see something in a person like me that was worth remembering. That somehow, my big dreams and unrealistic hopes, my fan letters and flowers, were all more than ways of fooling myself. They were more than ways of avoiding humiliation. They might turn out to bring me dignity, even if I didn't yet understand how.

On the night of Madonna's *Will & Grace* taping, I saw a man off to the side who looked familiar, and I kept wondering where I'd met him. I asked Jamie the publicist who it was, and he said, "He's Debra's husband. He's a writer. Used to be an actor."

I asked his name, and Jamie said, "Daniel Zelman," and I seized up a little bit inside.

In 1994, when I was in seminary, toward the end of a period when I had been so consumed by attempts to keep awareness of my sexual desires at bay, and so fearful of what might happen if I allowed myself to pursue the dreams my heart refused to stop producing, I fell into a deep funk that lasted more than a year. Sleeping ten hours a day and skipping classes were not addressing my problems effectively, and so a friend who knew I was having a hard time (and, as it turned out, knew why—even though I hadn't told her) suggested that I go to New York and see a play. I told her it was a nice idea, but I didn't have any money, and I didn't even know what I would want to see if I could afford to go. The next morning, tickets to both parts of *Angels in America* were in my mailbox at the campus center.

At the theater, a slip of paper in my Playbill announced that Daniel Zelman, the understudy for the part of Joe, would be playing the role that day.

Among the many stories in that play, Joe's was the one that stood out for me. He is a married Mormon who, upon discovering his lust for men, finds his faith gradually reduced to a convoluted exercise in self-denial. Joe never becomes comfortable enough with his desires to let them be transformed into real love with another man. At the end of the play, when most of the rest of the characters are gathered around the Bethesda Fountain in Central Park, Joe is absent and unacknowledged.

I couldn't stand that—because erasing Joe was like erasing me. When Joe was onstage, he brought to life a struggle that had been trying to gain centrality in my life for a long time. I had never seen a believer grapple with being gay. I had never seen anyone come out and try to stay true to who he had been before. Joe's failure did not make the struggle look appealing, but he did make it look necessary, if only to be sure of not ending up like him.

Angels in America was lightning on the fears I had kept hidden in the dark. Riding the train back to Princeton that night, I was exhilarated because I'd been found by this play, but I was also scared because I didn't know who I could talk to about it. I still didn't feel safe talking to the friend who'd given me the tickets, so when I got home, I stayed up late in the night writing a letter to Daniel Zelman to tell him how the play had moved me. I wrote that I didn't need for him to respond, that I just needed to tell someone what I was thinking. It was the last fan letter I ever wrote, and it was, perhaps, the only one I ever wrote simply because I needed to say something and thank someone, and not because I wanted something.

That night, on the set of *Will & Grace*, I felt that I should keep my mouth shut about what Daniel Zelman meant to me—I'd learned, repeatedly, there was no need to freight my work life with personal stories about my experiences as a fan—but I couldn't help telling Jamie, "I saw Daniel Zelman in *Angels in America* on Broadway, and it was one of the turning points in my decision to come out. It changed my life."

As I was talking, Jamie made a little O with his mouth; his eyebrows shot above his glasses frames, and then he grabbed my arm and marched me toward Daniel, as I was saying, "You don't have to do this . . ."

"Are you *kidding*?" Jamie said. "Babe, this is *great*!" Then: "Daniel! Daniel! Michael saw you in *Angels in America* and you *changed his life*! I'll be right back!" And he walked away.

Daniel, understandably, looked a little startled, and I smiled meekly and said, "It was a great performance," and we made small talk. I asked what he was writing, and he said, "A few things." We watched the cast shoot a scene.

As soon as the scene shifted, I looked up and there was Jamie at my side, this time with Debra: "Debra! Debra! Michael saw Daniel in *Angels in America* and it *changed his life!*"

"That's wonderful," Debra said in the polite and cautious tone that she had used to describe her encounter with Chad.

I wanted to vaporize. "Um, yeah, it was. I was a student at Princeton Seminary, and I actually wrote you a long fan letter, and—"

Debra: "That was *you?!*" Her eyes got huge, her shoulders tensed, her head tipped back. It was like a big ghost had flown down and we were all inside.

I felt elated and afraid, and my instinct was to question. I was covered in goose bumps: "Oh, come on. Please don't bullshit me. You couldn't possibly remember—"

"No!" she said. "We were together, even then, and I remember so clearly, reading that letter out loud in our tiny little apartment. How many fan letters from *Princeton Seminary* do you think *Daniel Zelman* got, as an *understudy?* And now you're here. Writing about me."

"*Freaky!* This is *so freaky!*" squealed Jamie, like he'd just seen a flash of underpants.

Something was happening. Something breaking, something building, my eyes stinging, and I smiled. Debra reached out and touched my right hand, the one I used to write five thousand fan letters, and it calmed all three of us down. "That was an amazing letter," she said.

Daniel said, "That was a good letter."

They didn't look or sound afraid of me, the way they'd looked just a minute before. They talked to me like I was someone that they knew, even though I wasn't. So we three clung for just a second to this tiny memory: a slippery plank that had popped up in the middle of the ocean, providing us a moment of security and relief. A lot is lost in people storms. Some is made there, too.

5

Hollywood Heritage

WEARING A BLACK STRAW hat, rose-colored glasses, and gold hoop earrings, historian Lisa Mitchell stepped to a podium in the Hollywood Heritage Museum, which occupies the barn where, in 1913, Cecil B. DeMille made his first movie, produced by (among others) Paramount Pictures founder Jesse Lasky. Her audience—a few dozen movie fans whose collected trivia knowledge, if written down, would fill so many books that you could probably never read them all—sat on folding chairs and listened with rapt attention as she spoke, in a voice as soft and warm as an angora sweater. "Well, we're all here in The Barn. And, as most of us know, it was originally on the Paramount lot when it was over on Marathon—the Paramount that we all know and love and remember from *Sunset Boulevard*. Stars of the time would pass by The Barn. The stars were certainly aware of The Barn. Then after a day of hard labor in front of the camera, they would walk out the Bronson Gate—the same Bronson Gate that you know from *Sunset Boulevard*. And they would think maybe now they could go home and rest. But that wasn't true. Because they would have to encounter a teenaged boy on roller skates, with a great big overcoat that didn't fit him very well, with a belt on it, and a string attached to the belt, and on that string was a camera. And in his pocket was an autograph book. And he would pester anyone he could, over and over again, to get them to sign his book, and to pose with him for a picture . . ."

Ray Bradbury stood, leaning on a metal walker. The white wisps of his floating hair trailed off in all directions, and his squinting eyes looked flat behind thick glasses with heavy, rectangular, brown frames. Short of breath, he said, "When I roller-skated to Hollywood that first day in April 1934, I was hoping to see famous people. And by God, standing there on the front steps of Paramount was W. C. Fields. Well, I roller-skated up to Fields and I said, 'Can I have your autograph?' He signed and he said, 'There you are, you little son of a bitch.'" He crossed himself. "And I was knighted."

Thanking Lisa for her introduction, he said, "I've got to tell you a story about her. I took her to a screening of a W. C. Fields film about twenty-five years ago . . . On the way home, Lisa was driving. And it suddenly popped into her head, she said, 'Where was it, where you met W. C. Fields?' I said, 'Well, turn here, turn there, and we ended up on Marathon Street in front of Paramount Studios. She said, 'Where was it? Show me the exact spot.' So we got out of the car, and I pointed to the steps in front of Paramount. And she took me in her arms. And she hugged and kissed me. And she said, 'Now, where did you see Fred Astaire and Ginger Rogers?' This got very interesting."

Betty Lasky, Jesse's daughter, who sat in front of me, began to giggle.

"I said, 'Around the block, onto Gower, and a block up, in front of RKO.' And we got out of the car, and she said, 'Where were you?' And I said, 'Right there,' and she took me in her arms and kissed me again."

Marjorie Fasman, Sol Lesser's daughter (he produced *Our Town*, and the original *Tarzan*), who sat next to me, joined Betty Lasky's laughing.

"She said, 'Now where was it you saw Ronald Colman?' 'Down at Columbia Studios in 1937 when he was making *Lost Horizon*.' So we drove to Gower near Sunset, got out of the car, and I pointed to the entrance of Columbia Studios, and she kissed me and hugged me for a third time."

He winked. The crowd was his.

"Now, *that* is a Hollywood historian for you."

Hollywood Heritage is a nonprofit organization that works to preserve architectural landmarks associated with the early film industry and its pioneers. The group's supporters include children of the first movie moguls, Hollywood mayor Johnny Grant, director Don Roos (*The Opposite of Sex*), writer Budd Schulberg, and dozens of passionate fans who've packaged their ardor in 501(c)(3)s. One, Robert Nudelman, is the director of project development for Debbie Reynolds's movie memorabilia museum. Another, Miles Krueger, lives in a West Hollywood duplex that doubles as a museum called The Institute of the American Musical. ("I'm not an atheist," Miles told me. "I believe in Judy Garland.")

Although the group has played a critical role in restoring the El Capitan theater and many other buildings, Hollywood Heritage fights to save bricks and mortar in order to preserve a certain notion of the city's emotional architecture, too. At monthly meetings, the group's well-known members give fans the gift of their memories and enjoy the treat of soaking in these fans' informed and endless attention spans. They're united by a nostalgic confidence that the business of Hollywood is, or ought to be, essentially personal. As Ray Bradbury averred, in his adenoidal tenor, "All of you who are here tonight, we are the lovers, aren't we? And the Hollywood people take advantage of us. They know that we're in love with movies, and so when we go in to make a deal, they offer us ten cents, don't they? And if we get them up to twenty, we're lucky. I've spent a lifetime trying to hide my love when I go in to meet producers or directors. But it's hard to do."

After his speech, I asked Lisa Mitchell if she remembered anything else from the night that Ray had described. She said, "When we would stop in front of a studio and we would get out, I would say, 'Paramount'—I would speak to the studio—I would say, 'Paramount, remember when this boy couldn't get in the gate, and this boy was standing there on the outside? *This is that boy.*'"

After my first Hollywood Heritage meeting, while reading the group's monthly newsletter, I noticed a familiar name: an old pen pal from my teenage years, a man named Phil who, in 1985, answered an ad I'd placed in an autograph collectors' magazine seeking the address of Grim Natwick, the animator who'd created Betty Boop. For tat, Phil asked if I had the address of Herb Morrison, the radio announcer whose broadcast from the *Hindenburg*'s 1937 crash became the most famous account of the tragedy. In his letter thanking me for that address, he wrote, "Like you, Michael, I collect in all areas and *do not limit* my interests, there are so many different people that have accomplished so much and given to the world through their various talents. Once you get started it is hard to *stop!*" He worked in a photo lab, where he made an eight-by-ten of the *Hindenburg* explosion for me to send to Herb Morrison to be autographed. Beneath his signature, the old newsman wrote, "Oh my God, Charlie! Their hair is on fire! Oh, the humanity!"

Every weekend, Phil and his identical twin brother, George, would go to Hollywood yard sales where they found treasures that Phil enthusiastically described to me in letters, which always came in big envelopes stuffed with dozens of glossy photos of famous people that he made in the off-hours at his job. Phil was in his thirties then, and to me he had the mystique that distant pen pals always do. I remember being shocked to learn that he had curly red hair when he sent a picture of himself, posed with his Chihuahua Rita ("so named for *Rita Hayworth!*").

Since I'd stopped collecting, I hadn't been in touch with Phil, so I called him, and he invited me to the Valley for a visit. A bachelor, he lives with his eighty-six-year-old mother, a collie, and six cats in the house where he grew up. The hallway outside his bedroom is lined with rows of dolls, which both he and his mom collect: the original Charlie McCarthy, the original Mickey Mouse, Pee-Wee Herman, Chatty Cathy after Chatty Cathy after Chatty Cathy. I sat on his narrow bed, against a wall covered with framed autographs of everyone from Dorothy Stratton to the Marx Brothers, and Phil showed me a vintage shot of George Reeves as Superman, shown full-length, hands on hips, boldly signed. "This is my ultimate," he said. "This would be going in my pyramid with me." He traded two Jean Harlows for George Reeves because he loves George Reeves more than any other star. "I don't know why. Just, Superman. He was Superman." He still kicks himself for missing a chance to buy the original Superman suit for

$5,000, but, as he handed me a snapshot, said, "At least I did get my picture taken in it."

Phil's hair had turned almost completely white in the years since I'd known him, and he had grown a beard because "I was watching *Robin Hood* with Errol Flynn, and it seemed like the thing to do." It's been hard, as he's grown older, because so many of his friends have gotten married and had children, and "people like my friend Barbara, she's a nurse, they don't understand the collecting. So most of my best friends are collectors." I asked him who his best friends are, and there was a long pause. "God, I don't know. My friend Barbara, I guess. I guess Barbara. And then . . . A few people from work I see, but I don't know. I don't know. It's hard to say. You! I think you're a good friend. I don't know. It's really, you don't have a lot of friends in this world."

Even collecting doesn't give him the joy it used to. He still goes to the yard sales, but "with eBay, everybody seems to know what things are worth these days. It's really tough." He also goes to the Hollywood Collectors' Show at Beverly Garland's Ramada Inn, but he does not like what he sees there. "They had Laverne and Shirley there, they saw someone taking their picture a few tables away, and they said, 'Hey! That's ten dollars!' What is that *about*? What has it come to? Autograph collecting, so much of it, is not friendly anymore."

He wishes things were like they used to be. "I don't see what these new people have, these Britney Spears. I just don't get it. I will not watch *Entertainment Tonight*. I don't care what Tom Cruise ate for dinner, or who his latest this or that is. I mean, who cares? To me, all these people are so artificial."

"More artificial than Rita Hayworth?" I asked.

"I don't know." He showed me a still of Rita (born Margarita Carmen Dolores Cansino) from the "Put the Blame on Mame" number in *Gilda* (in which her voice was dubbed by singer Anita Ellis), inviting me to "look how beautiful this is." I kept my parentheticals to myself; I knew that Phil already knew them. On the *Gilda* still, I did point out a faint line along the edge of Rita Hayworth's body, where her figure had been trimmed to make her shape more perfect. Admiringly, untroubled by inconsistency, he said, "They did all kinds of things like this, to make stars look better than they were."

He asked about my work: what celebrities I'd interviewed, and if I ever get their autographs.

"You don't even want to? Never?"

He let that sink in.

"You mean it just completely went away?"

It didn't go away, I told him. "With what I do for work, I probably spend more time thinking about stars than you do."

Though I don't ask stars for autographs anymore, as a journalist writing profiles of them I have continued a similar, and similarly cyclical, occupation. I imitate intimacy with famous people, to create documents that suggest I am the kind of person who's worthy of attention, which brings more assignments to imitate intimacy with famous people, and so on. The people whose attention I need now are editors who give me work, not little old ladies who feed me sherbet and cookies while they page through my photo albums; and since my interactions with celebrities are in real time, not in letters, I have learned to meet stars knowing that their mystery and beauty will likely prove neither mysterious nor beautiful. Still, the pattern is the same.

A person's sense of identity, Garry Wills has written, "is based on the experience of perdurance through shifting circumstances, and since all actual situations up to the present were, by definition, *past* situations, identity always has to be sought in the past. That is why continuing scrutiny of the real past is so important to human growth."

On the morning that Ronald Reagan's casket was put out for viewing at the Ronald Reagan Library in Simi Valley, I drove two hours through a landscape so hazy it was practically black-and-white and took my place in line with thousands who had made the same trip.

Several hours later I entered the room where the military honor guard stood watch over the coffin on a bier draped with black silk. Photographers along one wall of the room clicked photos of the mourners as we walked alongside the casket, and after a moment's distraction at the cameras— did I want to look so moved that someone would put my picture in the paper, or so unmoved that they wouldn't?—I concentrated on the coffin and felt unsettled, but not exactly sad. And then, a mild, freeing shock: there was the figure who'd focused my boyhood dreams, a corpse in a box. I imagined its shape in the dark, sealed space.

In front of me a man with a crew cut squared his feet to the casket and saluted. Behind me a plain man and woman clung to one another, faces wet with tears. Earlier, when I'd asked some of the people standing in line with me why they had come here, they had said, "This is history," and, "It makes you part of history." When I'd asked what that meant, they'd said, "It's big. You want to be a part of it," and, "Look at all those cameras, you don't think this is part of history?"

When I was a child, I was crazy about Ronald Reagan because he was both the grandpa I wished I had and the ideal man I longed to be: a dream of perfect kindness, confidence, and strength. When I grew up, I learned that no such person exists and came to understand my fantasies about him as echoes of my hero's own fantasies about himself, and about America.

Ronald Reagan's account of his personal history was riddled with false memories and fictional events, a self-deception perfected during his years in Hollywood. He also purveyed myths about America's history and character—fundamentally, that American capitalism is based on, and requires for survival, the robust individualism that Ronald Reagan purported to embody.

Many Americans still accept such myths as history, for some of the same reasons that fans idealize stars: these fantasies allow us to believe that individuals are more powerful, and our society is more benevolent, than is actually the case. People idealize stars because we want to believe human beings can throw off the past, transcend social hierarchies, and be reborn as singular selves whose importance cannot be denied.

To accept the impossibility of such fantasies would be traumatic. So we don't admit that faux-Anglo "Rita Hayworth" was a creation of shady sugar daddies and moguls. We don't accept that simple Mary Hart is a smart business-woman who swims with the sharks. We don't allow that the stars of *C.S.I.* are tools for "sellin' soap," as one actress in that franchise described her job to me. Instead, we imagine a world where Madonna's happiness is more complete than ours, a world where Dolly Parton could someday be our friend.

These are falsehoods and evasions, and they articulate a vital need. We work in an economy where everyone, it seems, is finally a cog. All too often, daily life makes us feel insignificant. But our culture is still haunted by the notion that a man was God; we have an ineradicable longing to believe that individuals are unimpeachably significant. Fandom helps give hope to that longing—and at the same time, reveals its sadness and absurdity.

Fans express their longing in many ways. The simplest and most common is our enjoyment of trivia. A fan's memory is full of flecks of facts and faces that seem to lead nowhere and prove nothing of themselves, except that we care about them—and apparently, that we care about them so deeply that we preserve them without consciously deciding to, even when we'd rather our brains use that space for other things. No one ever *tried* to remember the plot of a *Brady Bunch* episode.

Many of my most satisfying discoveries in Hollywood have been absolutely trivial. Like when Molly Ringwald disclosed in an e-mail to me that in *Sixteen Candles*, "Jake Ryan was *almost* Viggo Mortensen. (My first choice.) He kissed me in the audition and almost gave me a heart attack." Or when I asked Missy Elliott if she ever wrote a fan letter as a kid, and she laughed like she was busted: "I used to write Michael and Janet a whole bunch of fan mail. It got to a point where I started telling them that I had cancer, I was in a wheelchair." Or when I asked Will Smith if he remembered the first time anyone asked him for his autograph, and he said, "It was about thirty days after my first record came out. My grandmother got a copy of it and asked me to autograph it. The first time, you stand there and you're like, What do you write? Do you write your whole name? Do you write your real name? Do you write your stage name? And how do you make it? What does it look like?" Or when I asked Tom Cruise the same question, and he screwed up his face and looked away, crossed his arms, put knuckle to chin, shook his head, and finally, sounding a little sad, came out with "No, I don't, actually."

Though fandom is full of falsehoods and evasions, it is built from facts. And if you're interested in making sense of the role that fame has played in your personal history, a casual inventory of the Hollywood trivia stored in your brain would be as fun a place to start as any. Think of the stupidest, silliest stuff you know about stars. What does it mean that you know Mark Wahlberg has three nipples? What does it mean that you still remember Simon LeBon's birthday? That you still know the theme song from *Sanford and Son*? Maybe you'll find out that you're a little kinkier than you usually admit, or more romantic. Or get a clue about why you're dating that guy all your friends say is a dope. Or why you haven't had a girlfriend in two years. Or decide you're glad you sold your electric guitar. Or decide to buy one.

Think of the wildest dreams about stars you've ever had. Think about the most painfully embarrassing things you've done, or wanted to do, or seen other people do, when you got near stars. Maybe you'll decide Dolly Parton's really not worth your time if she can never be your friend. Or maybe you'll decide that you can believe you have a relationship with her, and know that you don't have a relationship with her, and that she's just a simple country woman, and that she's an ice queen, *all at the same time.*

Maybe you'll decide this kind of play of fantasy is what celebrities are *for* and, by consciously making that decision, find yourself totally cool and unembarrassed about still being a goon for Shaun Cassidy or Farrah Fawcett. Enjoying, even loving, the most inane, inconsequential stuff you've ever done and dreamed. More aware of what kinds of beauty or achievement you value. A little tougher about the difference between fake and real, in parts of your life where that difference really matters.

That day you met Ringo Starr, were you with some friends? Give them a call. See what they remember, too. Memory surprises as much as fantasy. Maybe more so.

The second time I got Ronald Reagan's autograph I was seventeen, working as a volunteer at a fancy fund-raiser on the floor of the Chicago Board of Trade, where, after having my picture taken with him, I handed him the letter I'd received in thanks for the Christmas ornament I'd sent for the White House tree and asked him to sign it. Glancing at the letter, he raised an eyebrow and chuckled, "I already signed this!"

"No," I said, "I believe that was your autopen, Mr. President."

Putting his authentic signature beneath his fake one, he said, "Well, I guess you know better than me."

After I saw Ronald Reagan's coffin, I called my dad and we reminisced about the time I told the president I loved him, and the time our congressman got his autograph for me, and the time I got his autograph myself. I said,

"Remember when he thought the fake signature was real, and I said it wasn't, and he said, 'Well, I guess you know better than me'?"

My dad, who was also there, said, "That's not how it happened. Reagan said, 'I already signed this,' and you were quiet for a second, and then you said, 'Then could you please sign it again?'"

Amazed, I disagreed. I told my dad that I remember that exchange as clear as yesterday. Later, though, I started wondering if Dad was right. After all, he, as a father, was focused on his son; and I, as a fan, was focused on my star. The exchange that I remember is more than plausible: its last line captures Ronald Reagan's careless affability; it's the kind of thing he would have said. The exchange my dad remembers is just as credible: its last line captures the gentle persistence with which I've always approached the famous, although my own memory adds the cheekiness that drove me, too.

In their way, both memories are truthful, but only one of them can be accurate. I'll never know for sure what words were said the day I finally met my dream. One thing I do know: that autograph is real.

ACKNOWLEDGMENTS

For their help in making this book, I thank Jon Barrett, Kathy Belden, Marian Brown, Sara Bullard, Bunny, John Case, Dante Di Loreto, Colin Dickerman, Eve Gerber, Sue Good, Angela Gross, Joseph M. Gross, Chris Harris, Amanda Katz, Hilary Liftin, Michael Lowenthal, the MacDowell Colony, Sara Mercurio, Kathleen Miller, Doug Patch, Laurie Pike, Bernard Prusak, Elyse Rubin, Lori Seid, Karen Shepard, Tai Uhlman, Elizabeth Van Itallie, Lydia Wills, Steven Wilson, Jason Yarn, and the newspaper and magazine editors who helped shape early versions of some of the stories told here.

A NOTE ON THE AUTHOR

Michael Joseph Gross has written for the *New York Times*, the *Boston Globe*, the *Atlantic Monthly, Entertainment Weekly, Elle*, the *Nation*, and many other magazines and newspapers. He won PEN/New England's 2002 Discovery Award for nonfiction. He lives in California.

A NOTE ON THE TYPE

The text of this book is set in Linotype Sabon, named after the type founder Jacques Sabon. It was designed by Jan Tschichold and jointly developed by Linotype, Monotype, and Stempel in response to a need for a typeface to be available in identical form for mechanical hot metal composition and hand composition using foundry type.

Tschichold based his design for Sabon roman on a font engraved by Garamond, and Sabon italic on a font by Granjon. It was first used in 1966 and has proved an enduring modern classic.